GOD
MONEY

"EMPOWERING CHRISTIAN ENTREPRENEURS TO CREATE WEALTH AND DISCOVER GOD'S ABUNDANT PLAN FOR THEIR LIVES THROUGH ENTREPRENEURIAL SUCCESS, STEWARDSHIP AND SPIRITUAL GROWTH."

CREATED BY

GOOSE SUSSI

MY SECRET WEALTH CREATION FRAMEWORK INSIDE

"YOU WERE BORN ON PURPOSE AND FOR A PURPOSE"

-GOOSE SUSSI

CHAPTERS

1 THE GOD MONEY MINDSET 5

2 MONEY 35

3 TITHE 53

4 SNOWBALL BAD DEBT, CREDIT SCORE & LEVERAGE CREDIT 75

5 THE GOD MONEY 10% 20% 70%FRAMEWORK 95

6 INCREASE YOUR INCOME 109

7 ASSET ACCUMULATION........................... 123

8 INCREASE YOUR INCOME "AGAIN" 155

9 THE GOD MONEY 10% 40% 50% FRAMEWORK 175

10 YOU ARE A ONE OF ONE 187

WHAT READERS ARE SAYING ABOUT THIS BOOK!

Sydney Robinson

Christian Author & Eunturpenure:

"All that I can say is the word AMAZING... this book was absolutely amazing!!! I literally felt the Spirit of God moving in me as I read it and by the time I finished it (actually before I did), I was led by the Holy Spirit to do the one thing that I refused to do for over a decade... Tithe. I didn't do it because I wanted anything, nor because I felt that I "owed money to God". I did it because I knew (now) in my heart that it's a foundational principle that is true. Additionally; I found the wisdom Goose shared regarding money via that 10/20/70 concept to be not only achievable but, it's so simple my pre-teens could do it. The examples he shared from his own life regarding credit restoration, real estate investing and business development were valuable beyond words. Even the examples he shared of ways to expand your income were simple to follow and applicable but more, they're priceless. I've been in financial services for over 15yrs and felt that the wisdom, guidance and action steps in this book to be not only smart to follow but PARAMOUNT to your overall financial success. I don't know how long Dave Ramsey plans to "carry the torch" but one thing is certain; God has given Goose his very own!!!"

Michael Boerner

Founder of Engage Technologies & Mission 17 Ministries:

"Goose Sussi's 'God Money' illuminates the complex interplay between spiritual truth and economics with rare clarity and balance. Goose and his wife Kelsie exemplify a harmony of faith and finance that speaks intensely to the heart of Christ-centered stewardship. Goose's gripping personal journey informs his profound insights, offering a guiding light for those seeking to infuse their financial and entrepreneurial endeavors with deep spiritual integrity."

Natalie Hernandez

Owner of Commercial Northwest Property Management & Host of Beyond Rich Podcast:

"Amazing intro! I can feel the Spirit behind each word. You want people to be free! To be prosperous in all their ways. To be a joyous example of God's Goodness! I am blessed to play a part in your ministry. Thank you for including me. It is an honor."

Erika Ulrich

Christian Entrepreneur & Principle of Capital Christian Academy

"I loved it. My favorite nuggets were:

The part about you vs. you and God in the "create over compete" section I love that phrasing. Also loved the phrase "race to the bottom with price" when you talked about how you set your sports bracing business apart. I've never heard that one before. So true. I loved how you explained abundance and prosperity and addressed some of the common concerns about the "prosperity gospel". I thought it was interesting how the Greek definition of prosper is so different from our dictionary. "To reach or attain" is so different than having a lot of money. You can "reach or attain" things that don't bring much money at all. Thinking specifically of my school project. This is a passion project God is helping me "attain" this goal and be prosperous in this endeavor because it means something to me (and to Him) and it has nothing to do with money. I know, however, that it will tee me up for future success because it blesses my community, brings new relationships, and it's a vision God told me to be obedient in. I just know that there will be more "prosperity" born out of this project in the future."

Matt Tucker

Principle Chair of C12 Form Idaho

"My biggest take away so far is how practical you make the principles. I think too many times we stay super theoretical and leave people asking, "Ok, but what do I do tomorrow?" Your book leaves them with clear steps, as well as clear convictions!"

Pastor Krist Wilde

Head Pastor of Capital Church in Meridian ID:

"Love your writing style! It's effortless and compelling. Your focus on stewardship is the fulcrum for everything else - I loved how you emphasized that.

Purpose is exactly what people in our cultural moment need to hear - we are starving for it. The first chapter speaks to that "felt need" perfectly!

I also love the staccato-style approach.. you offer bullet points for your God mind-set and then you give a fuller explanation later. Stylistically it's nice but more important it helps with inculcating the content!

Great job!! So proud! And I loved the first chapter! Thanks for letting me read it! Praying for God's continued blessing and abundance on it!"

INTRODUCTION

Congratulations and thank you for picking up this book! I mean that from the bottom of my heart! Words can not express how truly grateful I am that you decided to buy this book and make this investment in yourself. When you grow you can help those around you grow. I KNOW this book will serve you in every way.

My goal in writing this book is to share my GOD MONEY journey in building my financial empire the GOD MONEY way. So that you too can have the tools and strategies needed for you to be able to also build your God Money Empire. I want to help people discover and tap into everything God has in store for them and nothing less. If you take the tools and strategies from this book and apply them, your life WILL change! "For I know the plans I have for you" declares the Lord, "plans to prosper you and not to harm you, plans to give you hope and a future". I am a Christian businessman writing from my own personal experience. These strategies and tips in this book are God sent in one way or another. If you aren't a Christian, keep reading. This book is also for you and my hope is that along your journey you'll come to meet, see, and understand God better.

God has an amazing life for you, a life filled with joy, purpose, abundance and love. Yes this will look different for us all. This is not a book filled with "prosperity preaching" or things that sound good and might work, but this is a book filled with practical biblical strategies and God Money formulas that will help accelerate your wealth building journey and your ability to enjoy the life God has for you.

I must start off by letting you know I am not a preacher, I am saved by the grace of God, I am a husband, a father, a businessman, a dreamer, a friend, along with many other things. This book is the BluePrint on how I went from $4 to my name and a -$30,000 net worth at the age of 23 to a millionaire by the time I was 29.

I grew up in a family that didn't have much money. I was born in West Monroe, LA and 6 weeks later my mom, dad, and I left for Clarkston, WA where my grandparents lived. I am the oldest of 4 boys, my parents split when I was about 9, we grew up in and out of church. We had a household filled with love and encouragement, but no money. Money always limited everything we did. I moved 16 times before I got to college. I am not going to do a deep dive on all the details from my childhood and my upbringing, that will be in another book down the road.

"Our goal is to empower individuals to build a wealthy mindset, strengthen their faith, and increase their financial abundance in alignment with biblical principles. Through the sharing of stories, strategies, and practical insights, our goal is to inspire and equip people to use their finances in a way that honors God and transforms their lives and the world around them."

NOW LET'S DIVE INTO THE GOD MONEY BOOK!

1 THE GOD MONEY MINDSET

ROMANS 12:2

Do not conform to the pattern of this world, but be transformed by the renewing of your mind. Then you will be able to test and approve what God's will is—his good, pleasing and perfect will. (NIV)

JEREMIAH 29:11

"For I know the plans I have for you," declares the Lord, "plans to prosper you and not to harm you, plans to give you hope and a future." (NIV)

You are amazing. I mean it! Read it again. You are amazing! I know if you implement the strategies and mindset in this book, you will have a prosperous life that is full of meaning and blessings. Let's go!

Let's jump into this first chapter: GOD MONEY MINDSET.

I'm sure you have heard it before but it is worth repeating.... Your mindset matters! You need to understand this before you move forward in this book or even in your life! You are what you think about. If you think you are a failure and can't ever get ahead because you aren't smart enough or come from the right family, then you won't be successful. Not because these things might have some truth to them but because you believe them to be true. Likewise, if you are a confident person and know there is always a way to get something done or get to the next step, you will be successful.

There is a story about two sons that were raised by an alcoholic father. He wasn't ever around and when he was he would take out his frustrations of life on his two sons. Fast forward: one son became a homeless alcoholic and the other a highly successful businessman, loved by his community and walking in God's will. When the alcoholic son was asked why he turned out the way that he did, he simply said, "Because my father was an alcoholic." When the successful son was asked, "How did you turn out the way you did?" he answered, "Because my father was an alcoholic."

How can two men with the same environment, with the same father, with the same "disadvantages" end up with two completely different lives? One son became a victim to his circumstance while the other son saw an opportunity to become more, to be better, to change his life. The only real difference between these two sons was their mindset.
"Whether you think you can or you can't, you are right."
- Henry Ford

I love this quote by Mr. Ford because it shows you that your mindset matters, your decisions matter, and YOU matter, greatly.

One of my pastors from our local church, Pastor Mark, says this: "When you're born you look like your mom and dad; when you die you look like your choices." Let that sink in... So whether you had an amazing upbringing or the worst, you can decide today to truly change your life and live out the abundant life God has for you. Not one person has to get less so you can get more. God is the creator of all. There is no lack with God; if there was, He wouldn't be God.

Before you go any further you owe it to yourself to ask these questions: Why did I buy this book? What am I lacking in my life right now? What kind of future am I going to "end up" with if I don't make any changes? What price will my future self have to pay if my current self doesn't make an adjustment?

So much of winning and business and family and living out your purpose comes down to your mindset and your beliefs. I'm not talking about your belief in God but what you believe about you! You see, you were created in His image. You are a creator, you are creative, you are a builder, you are love, you are kind, you are all these amazing things that God is because that's how He designed you! So if you aren't "LIVING YOUR BEST LIFE" right now or things don't look like you thought they were going to look, that's 100% OK! If you woke up today, congratulations! God isn't done with you! You were created on purpose and for a purpose. My hope is that while you go through this book you will be able to not only get inspired but that you will also be able to see the person God created you to be.

I recently joined a Christian Business Forum called C12. It is amazing, to say the least. It is a Bible-led business forum that operates using the BaaM (Business As A Ministry) FrameWork. It helps guide you in how to love people through your business while adding value to the marketplace.

We are called to be servants, called to serve. The greatest leaders are great servants. If you own a company, then the better you love and serve your employees, the better your team and business will be! This all starts with your mindset, your GOD MONEY MINDSET.

The GOD MONEY MINDSET is being able to serve and love others like Jesus did while at the same time wanting money but not loving money. God has placed certain desires in your heart, desires that are strong. It's why you have that drive to become the best version of yourself that you can be, the version that God designed you to be. God is so stinkin' GOOD, He will let you settle at whatever level you decide to settle.

What areas in your life have you settled because you decided you didn't want to grow anymore? Do you still have that uncomfortable feeling knowing you aren't where you should be or could be? That could be those God desires He placed in you. It used to drive me crazy when authors or personal development coaches would talk so much about mindset and having your mindset right. I just thought it was fluff and I wanted to know, but how do you REALLY become successful? You have to understand what successful means... to you! Success for me is going to be different and look different than success for you. True success is becoming who God created you to be.

The GOD MONEY MINDSET is understanding that everything happens *for* you, not *to* you. It's understanding that God is in control of everything but you still have your role to play. You control two things and only two things on this planet: your Attitude and your Actions. Everything else is out of your control. This should be good news to you. Now you can relax, knowing you can't control the world. Just focus on those two things moving forward through this book and throughout your life. You can only control your actions and your attitudes.

The strategies in this book work; they have worked for me and they will work for you if you apply them. There is no magic pill here, however; get everything from this book you possibly can, apply it and then let God do His part.

We are called to be good stewards. There are so many different examples of this throughout the Bible. Having the GOD MONEY MINDSET means you steward what God blesses you with. This means everything: your time, your talents, and your money.

Steps to a Practical God Money Mindset:

Pray and think about the following concepts, then write down what you hear God telling you.

-Partner with God

What does this look like for you?

-Steward for God

What do you have that you can be stewarding better?

-Abundance over lack

What are limiting beliefs you have adopted that aren't true and how can you start to get rid of them?

-Create over Compete

In what areas have you been competing instead of creating and how can you start creating?

-You vs. You & God

What is something in your life right now you have tried to figure out but haven't been able to yet? Give that thing to God and do your part.

-Never Settle

What are ways you have settled and are no longer going to accept?

Now let's look more closely at each concept.

Partner with God:

What does this even mean? The faster you can realize that your life has two partners, the quicker you can start to live and build your God Money Empire. (Moving forward, every time I mention your God Money Empire I am referring to your abundant life with God, true prosperity and wealth in ALL areas of your life).

God is always going to do His part. Why? Because He is a promise keeper. It would go against His character if He lied—because He is God! So when God says something and makes you a promise, He WILL do His part. You also have to do yours, though. I often hear a lot of Christians say, "This is just the season God has me in right now" or "If God wanted me to have more or do more then He would let me" or "I have enough" or fill in the blank with any other Christian-sounding excuse you'd like. Unless God has specifically told you these things then it's just you choosing good over God's BEST for you. I once heard Dr. Dharius Daniels from Change Church say, "Sometimes God's plans are His preferences," meaning God has BIG PLANS for your life. "For I know the plans I have for you, says the LORD." So here is how amazing God truly is. He wants the BEST for you, He has already designed the BEST for you, He already has done His part for you. Your part is deciding you want what God has for you. Your part is walking in faith and acting like God is telling the truth. He loves us so much that He won't force us to do anything. He wants to save you but He won't even force salvation on you. It has to be your choice. It is 100% our choice every single day. When you decide to partner with God you are saying "I don't want my good, I want God's BEST" for my life."

Steward for God:

Stewardship is the responsibility that Christians have in maintaining and using wisely the gifts that God has bestowed. This ties into partnering with God because God's part is to be God and He has already blessed you. You woke up today, you are reading this book to change your life, and you are still alive, which means God still has plans for you! And He will continue to bless you!

When I was in elementary school my mom told me something that I think about to this day. She said, "Son, when you don't use the gifts and talents God has blessed you with, it is as though you are spitting in His face." Bold statement from my ever-so-loving mother; it meant something to me, even at that young age. (Thank you, Mom, for always loving me and believing in me. I love you!) Whatever God has given me and whatever He gives me, it is my responsibility to steward it well.

Luke 12:48 says, "To whom much is given, much is required." Please don't misread that... I believe this is saying with everything we have, we should be good stewards of everything, no matter how much or little. Not when you become a millionaire, *then* start giving or *then* start being generous or *then* start to care about others. When I was broke ($4 to my name and owed $30,000) I took God at His word in Malachi 3:10 and started tithing. God says, "Test me in this," so I did. I brought my tithe and by being obedient–NOT perfect– my whole world changed. I suddenly met my wife, door after door of opportunities started opening, relationships I was being introduced to completely changed, and more and more money started flowing in!

We have all been given much. It doesn't matter if it's your time, steward it well; if it's your talents, steward them well; if it's your money, steward it well. You are still alive, you have another day. What a gift! Steward it well!

Abundance over lack:

The definition of abundance is *existing or available in large quantities: plentiful.*

The definition of lack is *the state of being without or not having enough of something.*

You get to choose which one of these you want to focus on. How do you think God operates? Out of abundance or out of lack? Did God create some things or all things? Did He create some animals or all the animals? Do you want not enough or do you want plenty? Your answers to these simple questions will show you that abundance is possible. You just have to believe and have faith that it is possible for *you*! God wants His BEST for you, not necessarily what *you* think is good for you.

In the New Testament the word *abundance* means "exceedingly, very highly, beyond measure, more, a quantity so abundant as to be considerably more than what one would expect or anticipate." In 1 Corinthians

2:9 God promises us a life that is far greater than what we could have without him. "However, as it is written: what no eye has seen, what no ear has heard, and what no human mind has conceived- the things God has prepared for those who love Him." When we focus on who God is and what He has done and act like He is telling the truth, we are able to walk in this abundant life now. Living an abundant life starts with your mindset; once you are truly grateful for what you have, it allows mental space for you to become more creative and use the skills and talents God has blessed you with to build the life God has for you and to build the life you want.

Create over Compete:

If you are or were an athlete, you were taught and told to compete. I can hear so many of my coaches still to this day… you gotta compete! I played soccer, football, basketball, track and baseball growing up and got blessed with the opportunity to play D1 college football for the University of Idaho—go Vandals! I love sports and still love competing to this day. Competing looks different for me today, though. I truly am only competing with myself—who I was yesterday, last week, last year, and who I am today. That's it!

I am pushing to constantly grow into who God created me to be. I kinda have always been this way growing up—this mentality of becoming the best version of myself so that I could inspire and help others do the same. *The Science of Getting Rich* by Wallace D. Wattles put words to this mindset I already had; it helped me understand it better and allowed me space to build off this mindset. I recommend his book.

One of the things I got out of it was the concept of "create over compete." God is The Creator and we are made in His image; therefore, we are also creators. In Genesis 1:27 it says, "So God created mankind in his own image, in the image of God he created them; male and female he created them." Now I don't read this and think I can create the stars but I do read this and believe we are all creators on this planet and we can create things.

We have planes, cars, computers... just take a look around where you are right now and you'll see creation all around you. You'll see God's creations and you'll see what humans have created. When you know life is abundant and there is no lack, then you are able to create. When you can see there is always a way, and a problem is just a solution away, then you are able to create. You don't have to compete because you can create instead.

One of the companies my beautiful wife, Kelsie, and I own is a Medical Bracing company. Now we are NOT the only medical bracing company in the world. We aren't even close to the biggest. Other companies even carry some of the same products as we do. However, no other company has the team we do, no other company runs the way we do, no other company cares at the level we do, and no other bracing company loves the way we do.

We understand that if we focus on competition then it's just a race to the bottom with price. We aren't able to provide the level of excellence we are capable of when we are focused on competing rather than creating. When you operate from a state of creating you are able to walk in that abundant life God has for you. You are able to become who you were created to be. So make a promise to yourself that you will no longer be a competitor but instead you will become the creator God designed you to be.

You vs. You & God:

Now this is who you're competing against… you! Except you're not alone. See, when you partner with God, when you steward well, when you think in abundance, when you create over compete, you are able to take on the old you with the new you. You and your new partner, God, can do anything! Matthew 19:26 tells us that "Jesus looked at them and said, 'With man this is impossible, but with God all things are possible.'" So dream BIG and ask BIG! Protect your mindset. Feed your mindset. Grow your mindset. How do you do this? By getting around the right people, by reading the right books, such as this, by praying and hanging out with God.

God will give you strategies and open doors along the way. You don't have to be perfect, just obedient and consistent. Trust that God is telling the truth and have faith that His Great is far better then your good. When you have the God Money Mindset you are able to out-work, outgive, outsmart, out-prepare, out-invest, outlive, and out-build the old you. Remember you are born *on* purpose and *for* a purpose. You have everything you need to take your next step. God gave you big dreams. He didn't give your dreams to anyone else. So when people don't understand why you are wanting to change, why you are wanting to step into a bigger calling or do something bigger, just remember God gave you those dreams and desires. I tell you this because the people who will try to kill your dreams are those who have already given up on theirs. God is a promise keeper and He will always do His part. JEREMIAH 29:11 says "'For I know the plans I have for you,' declares the Lord, 'plans to prosper you and not to harm you, plans to give you hope and a future.'" (NIV)

God wants to prosper you and He will when you partner with Him. A lot of Christians don't like the word PROSPER; some even cringe at the thought of it. They instantly hear that word and think of the "prosperity gospel" and a list of unhealthy emotions towards the thoughts and ideas of more…. more money, more stuff, nicer cars and homes—these are all just material things.

Let's look at the definition of *prosper*.

Biblical definition-

Prosper: The word "prosper" in the Greek literally means "to help on the road" or "succeed in reaching."

Dictionary definition-

Prosper: succeed in material terms; be financially successful, to flourish physically; grow strong and healthy.

This has more to do with the position of your heart than any of these other things. You say God doesn't care whether you make $1,000,000 a month or live in a 10,000 sq. ft. home or drive a Lamborghini. He doesn't care if you have those things, but what He does care about is whether those things have YOU! We will get deeper into this later in the book but this topic is worth repeating because false beliefs like this will keep you broke and keep you away from going after the abundant life God has for you.

Let's take a look at the word *prosper* and words like it. *Prosper* is mentioned 104 times in the Bible while *Prosperity* is mentioned 121 times. Out of all these scriptures the general consensus is that God wants to prosper you. When you walk with Him, He can't help but prosper you. The faster you realize this and shift your mindset to this understanding, the faster you can start to see all the ways God wants to prosper you.
I believe prosperity isn't only in your finances. I believe it's having godly success in all areas of your life! The relationship I have with my wife, with my kids, and with my community, having a God-honoring business that is making a difference in the world, being healthy

and energized to live the abundant life God has for me… it's all of these things and more. If you only have some of these things you are on the right path, but don't settle for good when God has His best for you.

Never Settle

When you settle, your main focus is on you. Settling is one of the most selfish things you can do. When you settle, you decide you don't need or want any more. The world misses out and suffers when you settle. There is a huge difference between settling and being content with where you are in this season. I believe you can be content without settling.

Choosing contentment over settling in our pursuit of financial stability and abundance means finding deep gratitude and inner peace by aligning our actions with God's purpose for our lives. Contentment doesn't mean being complacent or passive; it's about appreciating what we have while being faithful stewards of our resources. It's understanding that our worth isn't defined solely by money or possessions, but by the joy of knowing and trusting in God. Settling, on the other hand, leads to compromise and accepting less than what we're capable of achieving. By embracing contentment, we free ourselves from comparison and materialism, and we become empowered to use our wealth to bless others and make a positive impact. Ultimately, true wealth is found in our relationship with God, and contentment guides us towards wise decisions and a heart of generosity.

I believe that the devil wants you to settle and to be okay with just enough. I have just enough food, just enough money, just a nice enough car, just enough time with my family, just enough time for my church and community…. Just enough! This is a dangerous cancer in our world. The idea of just enough is when you start to settle. When we lose track of God's will and start to focus on our own comforts, we settle. Who said you needed to be comfortable? Who sold you this lie? I'm not saying you shouldn't have the comforts of a full belly, a roof over your head and a 1996 Dodge Dakota that's paid for and runs just fine. I'm not saying these things are bad; I believe God created us for more than just enough because He is a MORE than enough God! Getting over this idea of just enough takes time and lots of prayer and focus. It takes a growing mindset. When God opens your eyes to what He wants to do through you and in your life for those around you, then it's easy to understand why we weren't created or designed to settle. This is just another reason why it is so important to get clear on your goals and what your God-given purpose is so you can lose this idea of just enough and settling. God wants us to be content and grateful but the devil wants you to settle. This is all part of your God Money Mindset and becoming more focused on the potential in who you were created to be than on just your comfort zone.

When you make the God Money Mindset shift you are letting God know you are available for Him to do amazing things through you. Your family and friends start to notice a change in you. You become a beacon of light to those around you. You are able to focus on being the creator and not the competitor. You are able to notice needs and figure out ways to fulfill them. You are able to impact your community and the world. The way you do all of this is by partnering with God. Become a steward of all He has given you– your talents, your gifts, your resources and more. Focus on God's abundant life for you and pay no attention to anything less. Choke out even the thought of lack in your life. You do this by paying attention to what God says about you and His plans for you. You need to focus on becoming the creator you are and get rid of this idea of competing with the world. You need to understand that it's now You & God, not just you, on this journey and NEVER settle but be content throughout the process.

So to summarize, consider these God Money mindset shifts:

-Decide you want God's best for your life

-Pray/Meditate on who you were created to be

-Protect your mind by limiting negativity and increasing positivity

-Think about who benefits when you build your God Money Empire

Congratulations, you are now building your God Money Empire, and because you decided this is the life you want, you are able to bless those around you and show them they, too, can have a God Money life. Now that you understand the importance of your mindset and how to build your God Money Mindset, let's get into one of my favorite topics…MONEY!

2 MONEY

1 Timothy 6:10

"For the love of money is the root of all kinds of evil…" (NIV)

This is the verse that most Christians mess up about money. I've had more Christians and religious people try to tell me "Money is the root of all evil." I'm sure even if you aren't Christian you've heard this. It's NOT true. That's not what the Bible says. The Bible says "For the LOVE of money is the root of all evil" which is VERY different than money itself being the root. I'm very excited about this chapter because we are going to learn about money: what it's not, what it is, what to do with it and how to want it without loving it. We are going to expose money and how we live on an economic planet where money controls almost everything. It controls where we live, what we drive, what we eat, where we go to school, how much we give…. Without even recognizing it, it controls most of our daily decisions.

At the time of writing this book, 2023, there are some pretty shocking statistics that should wake us up!

-63% of households live paycheck to paycheck
-52% of households earn $75,000 or less annually
-10% of Americans collect 50% of all the income in the USA
-Top 1% of Americans control 31% of ALL wealth
-Top 10% of Americans control 68% of ALL wealth
-58% of Americans have less than $5,000 in savings

For this to be " the richest country in the world" this should prompt some serious questions. Based on these numbers we clearly have misinformation and horrible strategies on the topic of money. This is one of the reasons I feel so strongly about informing as many people as possible about the topic of money. I want to help millions of people understand God Money and get all of our proven strategies so that you can have a purposeful and abundant life, have the life God has for you.

We are going to continue working on our God Money Mindset throughout this book. One layer of that is our understanding and our new relationship with money. We will be learning how to shift our worldly understanding and relationship with money to a godly one. This is all needed for you to build your God Money Empire.

What is money? According to *The Oxford English Dictionary,* money is "a current medium of exchange in the form of coins and banknotes; coins and banknotes collectively." Throughout the Bible money and possessions are mentioned more than 2,300 times. Jesus spoke about money in roughly 15% of his preaching and 11 out of 39 parables, according to wealthwithapurpose.com. If Jesus thought it was that important, we should pay attention to it. We should probably understand it and we should have a biblical plan for it. Throughout the Bible and in life, money is neither a good thing nor a bad thing. It is unbiased and nonpartisan. It is nothing more than a tool!

Money is a TOOL

When I made this mental shift about money it opened my eyes to how much power I had been giving money– how I let it determine my day, my mind, and my life, without even realizing it. When I had money I felt great and like I had options; however, when I didn't have any I felt less than and stuck. Most of us learn from a very young age that things cost too much and rich people are greedy. Now I know this isn't true; however, this is our worldly introduction to money and wealth. It's scarce, it's hard to get, and you have to work hard to get it. None of this is true! Yes, you have to look for it, yes, you have to use your God-given abilities to create opportunities, and yes, work is required.

With this new fundamental truth that money is nothing more than a tool, you are able to get rid of a lot of the unnecessary emotions that can come along with money. If you had ten shovels and your church needed one, you needed to save two for a future project and you still had seven shovels to complete a project that only required five shovels... How emotionally attached to your shovels are you? You started with ten, were able to give three away and still had more than enough for yourself. If our feelings can be this way towards a shovel that is only a tool, then our feelings towards money can be the same.

Now say you have $10,000 and you give your church $1,000 and you put $2,000 away for a future project. You are still left with $7,000 that is more than enough to cover your current project. This example is the same. Both are about tools, but be honest, was it tougher mentally for you to give away your fake $1,000 to the church or one shovel? $2,000 put away into a future project or two shovels put aside for a future project? Most people have an easier time with categorizing the shovels in the right place but not the money. Why is that? When you have ten shovels it's easier to see how abundant your shovel game is and it's because of our understanding of the shovel. Most of us can agree that a shovel is a tool and it is useless until it is being used. Money is the same way. Money is useless until it is being used.

Money is a KEY

Money is a key to so many opportunities. A key is a tool to open doors. When you have a lot of keys you are able to open a lot of doors. When you have a lot of money you are able to open a lot of opportunities. Money is the key to higher education. If you pay tuition you are able to attend a college. Money is the key to being able to build a new church or orphanage to house the homeless. We all have God-given desires and God-given purposes. In order for you to become fully who you were created to be, you will need keys. You will need money. By praying and reading your Bible you are able to see God's plan for your life. You are able to develop a biblical relationship with money. You are able to pursue money in terms of needing it to further God's kingdom without falling in love with it in the process. If you've never been given permission to want money, or more of it, here it is. Go after it in a godly way. Keep focused on what you can *do with* the money instead of the money itself.

How many keys would you like throughout your life? How many experiences would you like to have in your life? How many people do you want to bless in your life? How big of an impact do you want to make in your life? These are all going to take money, and for as long as we live on this economic planet we are going to need money. So let's master money and not let it master us.

What is money for?

Money is to be used. It is useless until it is put to work. We have all heard the saying "Make your money work for you." This means putting your money into an asset that will earn more money. An asset is something that feeds your pocket. So if you go buy a new truck, that alone isn't an asset. However, if your new truck allows you to haul more or allows you to provide more value, in turn earning you more money, then it is an asset. One of our favorite ways to make our money work for us is through buying real estate. More on this later.

God Money Strategies

Since we live on an economic planet, money will be part of your life until we get to meet our Lord. Knowing this fact should help motivate you to start paying attention to money. You need a plan for your money. If you don't know what to do with your money then you're guessing, and you will be broke. There are people that make $500,000 a year and are broke and people who make $50,000 and are broke. So it can't be the money that is the problem. People think they have money problems… Yes, they do because they don't have a money strategy or plan. If you're broke it has more to do with your understanding of money and your current plan. This book will help change that. If you just apply this God Money strategy you will NEVER be broke again! That's right, never!

The person making $500,000 a year and the person making $50,000 a year are both broke because of their current money strategy. Both are spending everything they make. In America, every time we make more money or get a pay raise, we are conditioned to raise our standard of living! We buy the new house, the new car, the new boat, the new purse because we "deserve it." We have worked hard to get the raise so we treat ourselves. Now before you assume I'm saying you shouldn't have nice things or up your standard of living, please hear me out. In order to become truly wealthy you have to be willing to put leisure in its proper place. You have to be willing to stay disciplined long enough to actually see your God Money Empire building. You have to pay the price today so you can pay any price tomorrow!

Here are a couple of God Money Strategies that we will go into more deeply later in this book. The proven God Money Strategies that we used and use are the 10%20%70% and the 10%40%50% Rule.

You are going to take your income and put it into three different buckets. The first bucket is your 10% TITHE Bucket, the second is your 20% Save to Invest Bucket (STI) and the third is your 70% Live Off Bucket. The 10% Tithe Bucket is your tithe to whatever church you attend. If you aren't going to a church then find a church you want to support. God will do more with your 10% than you can do with your 100%. Your 20%

Save to Invest Bucket is for you to start learning how to be disciplined to build up some money to invest into assets that will pay you and build up your wealth. The commitment to these buckets at first is more important than the amounts in the buckets. You have to start the process. Your 70% Live Off Bucket is for the rest of your living expenses. More on this later in the book. If you use this God Money Strategy you won't be broke again. After you have mastered the 10%20%70% Rule and have figured out ways to increase your income (more on how to do this later, too) then you move to mastering the 10%40%50% Rule. You still have three buckets: tithing, save to invest, and live off. The only difference is now you are upping your Save to Invest Bucket from 20% to 40% and you're reducing your Live Off bucket from 70% to 50%. This is pouring gasoline on the fire and exploding your wealth building. You are maximizing your money and how it works for you, and reducing the time it will take to become financially free.

Money is to bless others, to make a difference, and to do the Lord's work. "More money will only make you more of what you already are." I don't remember where I heard that but it has seemed to be true for many years. If you are naturally a selfish person, chances are more money will only make you more selfish. If you are a naturally caring and giving person, then more money is going to allow you to do more of those things. Money just exposes who you are.

Poor vs. Rich vs. Wealthy People

Dr. Myles Munroe says:

> Poor people pursue money, rich people pursue things, wealthy people pursue purpose. Poor people spend money, rich people buy things, wealthy people grow money. Poor people talk about money, rich people talk about things, and wealthy people talk about ideas.

Isn't that interesting? Think about the last conversation you were in about money… What was the conversation based around? The lack or pursuit of money? Looking at new things to buy? Or was it about purpose? As you have already learned about the God Money Mindset it is very important that you surround yourself with people who, like you, are working towards big goals.

Nothing makes me disconnect quicker in a conversation than when someone is talking about the news, something negative, gossip, or complaining about money.

The front door to your house has a lock. You don't keep it wide open throughout the day so anyone or anything can just come in, so why do you allow this to happen in your mind? Our minds and our God-given abilities to think are so underrated and need to be taken seriously.

Be aware of the people you're spending the most time with because you are the sum of the five people you hang out with the most. So if those five people are always talking about the lack of money and how money is evil, then you need to make a decision about how important your God-given dreams are to you.

I mostly hang out with Christian millionaires. I don't purposefully seek them out; however, my awareness and EQ (emotional quotient/intelligence) of my environment helped create this circle. In a world full of mediocrity it is so refreshing to be able to talk about ideas and vision and purpose with other go-getters and kingdom builders. Now you don't have to be a Christian millionaire for me to hang out with you. However, if you have small stinkin' thinkin' and just like to gossip about others, then I can guarantee you we won't be spending too much time together. Don't take it personally, but we are just headed in two very different directions. You need to get like this when it comes to money also. Keep your priorities straight: Faith, Family, Finances, and go make as much money as God has given you the ability to make. Bishop Jakes once said, "I don't want anything God doesn't want for me… But I do want EVERYTHING He has in store for me." I love that quote because time and time again throughout the Bible God reveals Himself as a generous God and we are most like Him when we love and give. Money is just one of the things God wants to bless you with if you are willing to do your practical part. Be a good steward of what He has already given you, then ask Him for what you want and for His will to be done.

It's been my experience that you can't outgive God, and God's best is always way, way, way better than the world's good.

I do think targets and goals are important; however, I'm more excited about my God- given potential than any goal I can come up with. I do set goals and I do have targets for all areas of my life. Money should be viewed with this perspective as well. Rather than just trying to hit a number like $50,000 or $100,000 or even $1,000,000 earned in a year, go for your full earning potential. Get as far away from $0 as possible. By implementing my God Money Framework you will be able to do just this!

3 TITHE

MALACHI 3:8-12 NIV

8 Will a mere mortal rob God? Yet you rob me. But you ask, "How are we robbing you?" In tithes and offerings. 9 You are under a curse—your whole nation—because you are robbing me. 10 Bring the whole tithe into the storehouse, so that there may be food in my house. Test me in this," says the Lord Almighty, "and see if I will not throw open the floodgates of heaven and pour out so much blessing that there will not be room enough to store it. 11 I will prevent pests from devouring your crops, and the vines in your fields will not drop their fruit before it is ripe," says the Lord Almighty. 12 "Then all the nations will call you blessed, for yours will be a delightful land," says the Lord Almighty.

There is a lot of back and forth about tithing. I've had Christians tell me that tithing is only in the Old Testament and not in the new. To this I say, ask God and read your Bible. My understanding is that tithing is 10% of your income. God only asks for 10% even though He owns 100% of everything you have. How good is He?! When you can look at money the way God does, in percentages rather than amounts, you have a God Money Empire. Everything in my life changed when I started to tithe.

I grew up around church. Yes, we would attend every now and then and we would go to church camps in the summer but we weren't planted in a church. There is a BIG difference between going to church, or trying church, and being planted in a church.

I was taught it was good to give to the church. I don't recall ever having someone walk me through "the three different ways to give" but just that giving was a good thing to do.

A quick story on how I started tithing: I was 23 years old and not living like a Christian. I was doing things my way and not God's way. I was invited to a Wednesday night church group called GCD (Generation Church Downtown), at that time led by the youth pastor, Mark Francy. Pastor Mark is an incredible communicator and is one of the most anointed speakers I've ever heard. I started going to GCD every Wednesday. One night, the sermon Pastor Mark spoke on was about "Being a Generous Giver." I was a broke young 23-year-old bussing tables and learning how to sell RVs as a salesman. Pastor Mark's message all those years ago stuck with me: "The devil won't ask you to give to the church" and "Tithe where you eat." In other words, where you go to church or get "fed" spiritually, give there. God will use your money to bless others.

God can do more with your 10% then you could ever do with your 100%! I remember giving that night what little money I had in my pocket…I don't remember how much it was but I do remember giving out of a spirit of challenging God and not being a cheerful giver. I remember thinking "OK, God, you said give, prove to me you're real." God tells us in Malachi 3:10, *"Bring the whole tithe into the storehouse, that there may be food in my house. Test me in this,"* says the LORD Almighty, *"and see if I will not throw open the floodgates of heaven and pour out so much blessing that there will not be room enough to store it."* So I did just that. I tested Him. Supernatural opportunities started to suddenly appear. A few weeks later I started actually tithing 10% of my income and God began to move in ways only He could in my life. I felt the closest I've ever been to God. I felt His grace and His favor.

I was 23 and broke, both financially and spiritually. I decided to give my life to Him, get baptized, and start living the life He had in store for me rather than doing things my way. Shortly after that decision, I met the most beautiful girl on the planet, now my wife. I had job opportunities just falling into my lap. I was making more money than I'd ever made. I tested God and acted like He was telling the truth, and in return He blessed me with abundance. Now money isn't the only thing that comes from your obedience to God in tithing. You gain more peace, more enjoyment, and a godly perspective of His will and purpose for you. It's not all about money but it is part of it. God doesn't need or want your money or your tithe...He wants your heart.

Growing up, we didn't have much money, but I knew one day I was going to be rich because I knew what it was like to be broke. God blessed my obedience. I didn't become perfect, I became obedient. When you walk under His protection and follow Him, your life becomes abundant. I didn't say it becomes perfect but it does become more blissful. It becomes more purposeful.

We all need money, but when your focus is on money you won't ever get it; however, when you focus on God and His plans you will get more than you could ever dream of. The Bible says in 1 Corinthians 2:9 "What no eye has seen, what no ear has heard, and what no human mind has conceived— the things God has prepared for those who love him." In no way am I judging you for not tithing or giving to a church. All I want is for you to ask yourself how different your life could be if you did start tithing and acted like God is telling the truth. If He did it for me, I know He will do it for you. You are loved and He wants to bless you. Yes, you!

Tithing is a Discipline:

Tithing is a muscle that you have to work. You position your heart to be able to give when you are diligent in tithing, making it a norm. If you don't, you are missing out on God's best for you. Making more or less money does not imply that it will be easier or harder for you to tithe. In other words, if someone is only making $15 an hour while someone else is making $1,000,000 a year, some would argue it is easier for the millionaire to tithe than the person only making $15 an hour. It's easy to think this way because we are focusing on the amounts and not the percentages. God asks for a percentage, not an amount. In the Bible, the woman who gave her last two coins was judged to be more righteous than the man who gave much more. Why? The important thing wasn't the amount given, it was the heart attitude of the giver. The woman gave more out of faith than the man did. When you are tithing and giving to the Lord you should feel it. It shouldn't be so casual. This is why at church we give through an app called Push Pay; however, every Sunday when the offering buckets come around I get my phone out to tap the side of the bucket. I want to never get complacent in my tithing and offering. God is purposeful towards me. I want to be purposeful towards Him.

3 Ways to Give

FIRST FRUITS: Proverbs 3:9-10

9 Honor the LORD with your wealth, with the firstfruits of all your crops;

10 then your barns will be filled to overflowing, and your vats will brim over with new wine.

Genesis 4:3-5

3 In the course of time Cain brought some of the fruits of the soil as an offering to the LORD. 4 And Abel also brought an offering—fat portions from some of the firstborn of his flock. The LORD looked with favor on Abel and his offering, 5 but on Cain and his offering he did not look with favor. So Cain was very angry, and his face was downcast.

First fruits offerings are so powerful! You are truly giving out of faith. Our church does a first fruits offering at the beginning of the year. It's an amount of money you pray about to ask God how much you should give. Ever since my wife and I have started giving first fruits, we have always been blessed financially. God asked Cain and Abel for their offerings. They both gave, however Abel's offering was accepted and Cain's wasn't. Cain's offering wasn't the first fruit offering but Abel's was. Abel gave God the best he could while Cain gave God what he wanted to give. There is power in first fruit giving.

If you aren't a believer, keep reading. This book is loaded with practical money moves to help you build your God Money Empire. You don't have to be a believer to read this book or even become rich; however, when you partner with God you are able to accelerate your wealth building and your enjoyment level far beyond what you could do alone. I am sharing from experience and not theories. Pray about it and ask God to show you.

TITHE: Malachi 3:8-10

"Will a mere mortal rob God? Yet you rob me. But you ask, 'How are we robbing you?' In tithes and offerings. You are under a curse—your whole nation—because you are robbing me. Bring the whole tithe into the storehouse, that there may be food in my house. Test me in this," says the Lord Almighty, "and see if I will not throw open the floodgates of heaven and pour out so much blessing that there will not be room enough to store it."

I don't want to rob God of anything. God doesn't want my money, He wants my heart. The word *tithe* means a tenth. By tithing 10% of our income it constantly keeps us in check on how our hearts are doing. It exposes what master we are actually serving, God or money. And when there is increase, we still tithe. I don't want anything that He doesn't have for me, but I do want *all* that he has for me. Money is a flow. When you are able to keep the flow moving through you then you are able to get more. When you stop giving, you stop the flow of being able to bless others.

OFFERINGS: 2 Corinthians 9:7

Each of you should give what you have decided in your heart to give, not reluctantly or under compulsion, for God loves a cheerful giver.

Offerings are extra giving. You can also give your time away. Time to volunteer in helping the church or your neighbors. Helping clean up your community. This is when you feel God saying, "Buy the coffee for the person behind you" or throw a little extra on the offering plate if you know there is a summer youth camp coming up in your church and kids need scholarships to go. All the other opportunities to give at your church are ways you can participate in giving offerings. I know people who think giving to the turkey drive counts as tithing but it really doesn't. It counts as offerings. Again, please understand that God is after your heart, not your money. Opportunities to give back to God are more for you than they are for Him. He wants to bless you, and He wants to know you are a good steward of what He's blessed you with. When you show God your obedience in giving, He is able to bless you in ways you couldn't even imagine. So act like God is telling the truth when He says He wants to bless you.

GROSS INCOME VS. NET INCOME

Every time I mention tithe or tithing, I am talking about 10% of your income. Well, is that 10% of your gross income or net income? It's both! If I am a W2 employee then I tithe off the net income. If I own my business or am a 1099 earner then I tithe off the gross income. The way I look at this is that, as a W2 employee, the government gets your paycheck before you do. The government already takes "their share" out of your check, so you are left with your paycheck minus the government's taxes. So you would tithe 10% off the net. If I'm an owner and now I have more control as to how much tax I can choose to pay, then I get to tithe off the gross amount because I got my paycheck before the government did. To take it a step further, one of my wife's and my businesses is a real estate company. Real estate is where we invest most of our investment money; it's our favorite Asset class for many reasons that I will share with you later. If we sell one of our investment properties and make a profit from the sale and take those profits for our own use, then we tithe on those earnings; however, if we take those profits and just roll them into another investment property, then we don't tithe off that amount. Any time we have actual income, we tithe 10% of that income.

15 Scriptures on Tithes and Offerings

1 Chronicles 29:9

The people rejoiced at the willing response of their leaders, for they had given freely and wholeheartedly to the LORD. David the king also rejoiced greatly.

2 Corinthians 9:7

Each of you should give what you have decided in your heart to give, not reluctantly or under compulsion, for God loves a cheerful giver.

Acts 20:35

In everything I did, I showed you that by this kind of hard work we must help the weak, remembering the words the Lord Jesus himself said: "It is more blessed to give than to receive."

Deuteronomy 16:17

Each of you must bring a gift in proportion to the way the LORD your God has blessed you.

Hebrews 13:16

And do not forget to do good and to share with others, for with such sacrifices God is pleased.

Luke 6:38

Give, and it will be given to you. A good measure, pressed down, shaken together and running over, will be poured into your lap. For with the measure you use, it will be measured to you."

Luke 16:10

Whoever can be trusted with very little can also be trusted with much, and whoever is dishonest with very little will also be dishonest with much.

Malachi 3:10

Bring the whole tithe into the storehouse, that there may be food in my house. "Test me in this," says the LORD Almighty, "and see if I will not throw open the floodgates of heaven and pour out so much blessing that there will not be room enough to store it."

Proverbs 11:24

One person gives freely, yet gains even more; another withholds unduly, but comes to poverty.

Proverbs 28:27

Those who give to the poor will lack nothing, but those who close their eyes to them receive many curses.

Psalms 4:5

Offer the sacrifices of the righteous and trust in the LORD.

Proverbs 3:9-10

9 Honor the LORD with your wealth, with the firstfruits of all your crops;

10 then your barns will be filled to overflowing, and your vats will brim over with new wine.

Luke 12:34

For where your treasure is, there your heart will also be.

Matthew 6:31-33

31 So do not worry, saying, 'What shall we eat?' or 'What shall we drink?' or 'What shall we wear?'

32 For the pagans run after all these things, and your heavenly Father knows that you need them.

33 But seek first his kingdom and his righteousness, and all these things will be given to you as well.

Mark 12:41-44

41 Jesus sat down opposite the place where the offerings were put and watched the crowd putting their money into the temple treasury. Many rich people threw in large amounts.

42 But a poor widow came and put in two very small copper coins, worth only a few cents.

43 Calling his disciples to him, Jesus said, "Truly I tell you, this poor widow has put more into the treasury than all the others.

44 They all gave out of their wealth; but she, out of her poverty, put in everything—all she had to live on."

We are most like Jesus when we are loving and giving. When you can step out in faith and start tithing and giving, your life will change! God doesn't want your money, He wants your heart. When you can truly understand that money is more of your heart's position than anything else, you start to understand money on an entirely different level. You start to see it through the lens of Kingdom Vision and how much more you can do with money when your heart is positioned correctly. When you give, you are building a landing strip for God's blessings.

Remember God is a good father and He won't give you anything you can't handle, this also means money.

4 SNOWBALL BAD DEBT, CREDIT SCORE & LEVERAGE CREDIT

PROVERBS 22:7 (BAD DEBT/NON PRODUCTIVE DEBT)

The rich rule over the poor, and the borrower is a slave to the lender.

PROVERBS 22:26-27 (BAD DEBT/NON PRODUCTIVE DEBT)

26 Be not one of those who give pledges, who put up security for debts. 27 If you have nothing with which to pay, why should your bed be taken from under you?

ECCLESIASTES 11:1-2 (GOOD DEBT/LEVERAGE/ PRODUCTIVE DEBT)

1 Ship your grain across the sea; after many days you may receive a return.

2 Invest in seven ventures, yes, in eight; you do not know what disaster may come upon the land.

In this chapter we are going to focus on the proper way to use and leverage credit and your credit score, but before we jump into that I want to share a quick story about my personal credit score. Yes, I know there are a lot of Christians out there who say, "Debt is bad, never go into debt." However, just like anything, when you use something in the way it was intended, you can have great results. But if you use something in a way it wasn't intended, you can find yourself in trouble or it could create a bad scenario--not because the thing was bad but because you used the thing in a way it wasn't intended to be used. I'm talking about credit. More on this later in this chapter.

I have been on my own financially since I was 18 years old. Yes, my parents would occasionally fill up my car with gas or give me a few hundred dollars every now and then, but for the most part I was responsible for my insurance, phone bill, food, rent, everything you could think to pay for. That is no knock on my parents. I truly believe they did the best they could and honestly, the way I was raised is part of why I am successful today. Parents are the best (thank you and I love you both)!

I never had a credit card nor did anyone ever teach me about credit. I remember being in college and signing up for an Old Navy card. After charging a coat on it, I forgot about that card. The late payments soon went to collections and I started getting the collectors' phone calls.

I was broke with no real income so I didn't pay my bills. I figured they had my number, I didn't have the money I owed, they would call me back, and one day I should be able to pay them back. Now I know this isn't responsible thinking, but at the time I didn't care because I was uneducated on how important a credit score is and how it can be a tool to help you build wealth. "Ignorance is NOT bliss… it's expensive." You see, at that time of my life I just knew one day I was going to be rich and so I wouldn't need credit because

I would be able to pay cash for everything. I had no idea how I was going to pull this off, however; I just knew one day I'd be rich.

Little did I know the rich don't pay cash for things. They actually finance most things. They use leverage and credit instead of their own money. This is an important lesson to get and understand. Debt doesn't have to be your problem, it can be your partner. The rich understand that by going into debt they can buy cash-producing assets such as real estate that will pay them monthly and help build their wealth. I was 23 years old with $4 to my name and a credit score of 407 before I started to learn and understand what the rich do. So rather than trying to reinvent the wheel, I decided to study and use money like the rich do.

SNOWBALL BAD DEBT (non productive debt)

Definition: take all your consumer debts, write them down from highest interest rate to lowest, and start paying them off in that order.

I remember at 23 years old making a list of everyone I owed money to. I wrote down all the account numbers, the collectors' names, and the amount of my debt. I learned this technique from Dave Ramsey. Now Dave and I disagree on his debt theory. However, I do agree with getting rid of dumb consumer debt. The non-productive debt. There is such a thing as good/productive debt and bad/non-productive debt and the kind of debt that most people have is bad/non-productive debt. After my list was created, I called every one of the collectors and told them, "I don't have your money yet but I am working towards paying you off." This was a big step for me. I was 23 years old and finally starting to take full responsibility for my actions. I was no longer going to blame anyone else for my lack of wealth and fortune. My position at that time was all my fault. If you are buried in bad/consumer debt, I encourage you to do the same- make your list now. If you don't do this you will always be in bad debt and you will never get to build your God Money Empire. God has so many things in store for you but until you break free of the debt slavery you won't be able to tap into God's greatness for your life.

Proverbs 22:7

The rich rule over the poor, and the borrower is a slave to the lender.

One by one, I started to cross off the names on this list. I went from owing everyone money to owing no one money! This resulted in so much freedom, building momentum and belief that I could actually get out of this situation and take control of my life. After getting rid of the Bad Debt in my life it was time to learn about leveraging and credit score.

CREDIT SCORE

Definition: A credit score is a number from 300 to 850 that rates a consumer's creditworthiness. 300 being very low and 850 being perfect

Earlier, I mentioned that I had earned myself a 407 credit score. This is actually pretty tough to do. You have to throw away all of your bills every single month over a long period of time and maybe, just maybe, if you stick with it long enough, you will earn a 407 credit score... I had the credit guy on the phone tell me, "Congratulations, Mr. Sussi, you are in the bottom 7% of America." This is something you do not want! Trust me.

It takes time to rebuild your credit. Instead of building your wealth, you have to focus and waste time trying to get a good enough credit score so the bank feels comfortable about partnering with you on your investment deals. So I took my 407 credit score and started to talk to mentors around me about the best way to build my score. Over and over, people who were doing far better financially than I was told me I needed to get a secured credit card and get a car loan. A secured credit card is a credit card that is backed by real money that you give the bank to prove you can handle the responsibility.

I went to my local credit union and I gave them $500 to secure a $500 credit card. As long as you show you are using your "credit card," paying off the balance and not overspending, then you build the trust of the bank so they will be willing to give you back your initial $500 deposit in exchange for a real credit card with a $500 limit. This will increase your credit score if you have bad credit or if you have little credit history.

Now that I had a real credit card, it was time for me to get a car loan. I needed a car anyway. At the time, I was renting a 2000 Daewoo Nubira from my buddy for $100 a month. I always paid cash for my cars so I never had a history of car payments to help build my credit. The most expensive car I had ever purchased was a Dodge Dakota for $3,800.

I spent a day traveling to as many dealerships as I could. I would walk in and say, "Hello, my name is Goose, I have a 407 credit score and I need to buy a 4x4 truck and I need you to report my payments to the credit bureaus." I went to so many dealerships that day without any luck, but finally stopped at Joe's Hot Wheels 'N Deals. They had one truck, a 2002 Chevy 1500 long bed with 180,000 miles, roll up windows and no carpet on the floor. It was clean, all things considered, and it checked all the boxes of what I needed at the time.

It was a 4x4, they would report my payments to the credit bureaus, and it ran! After they ran my credit score they confirmed that I had a low score. It was now up to a 520 and I was pumped! That's better than the 407 I had had. The truck itself was around $8,000 and my interest rate for that truck was 28%.... Not 2.8% but 28%! To be honest, I didn't care. I was so excited that someone would actually finance me, and I understood this truck was going to get me closer to being able to build my wealth. Now most people would say there is no way I would pay 28% interest for an old truck. And you would be right in thinking that 28% is very high. However, my goal wasn't to own that truck or to pay 28% interest; my goal was to build my credit. If I had waited until I had a credit score of 650 or 700 I would have wasted years focusing on the wrong thing. The wrong thing to focus on is the high interest rate; the right thing to focus on is the fact that my credit score was growing. I was getting closer to one day being able to buy real estate and start building my God Money Empire.

LEVERAGE CREDIT

Definition: use borrowed capital (for an investment), expecting the profits made to be greater than the interest payable. Or to use (something) to maximum advantage.

GOOD DEBT VS. BAD DEBT

Some of you think all debt is bad. You've been led to think of all debt as a bad thing and that you shouldn't have any of it and you should try to pay off all your debts. In the Bible there are two kinds of debt, productive (good debt) and nonproductive (bad debt). Let's first look at debt and what it actually is. It's an absolute gift! Debt should be your partner, not your enemy. Debt is a tool, just like money is a tool. When used correctly, debt can accelerate your wealth building. Debt should work for you, not you work to pay off your debt (other than, of course, getting rid of your bad debt). I know what the Bible says about debt and you should, too. It says to "be the lender and not the borrower"; it also talks about not being a slave to debt.

If you don't believe in debt, then why do you have employees? Don't you have to pay them every couple of weeks? You owe them for the work they did. You are in debt to them. Not all debt is created equally. Which leads us to Good debt vs. Bad debt.

Good debt *feeds* your pockets, bad debt *eats* your pockets.

Good debt is vital to creating wealth and true financial freedom. Good debt would be for buying assets that pay you; bad debt would be that which you take on to increase your standard of living. Get so much good debt that it pays for your bad debts. A good business or cash flowing real estate is worth going into debt for! A new car just to get a new car is a waste and is bad debt. Study what the wealthy people of the world spend money on and what they go into debt for and why. Success leaves clues.

Now, fast forward a couple years: I'm married to my beautiful wife, Kelsie, I have a good credit score (mid 600s), and my wife and I are able to buy our first piece of real estate. We decided for our first home we would buy a duplex. We looked at a lot of homes and almost gave up on buying a duplex. Thank God we didn't, because buying the duplex was a key to building our God Money Empire.

Buying the duplex was actually an asset and not a liability. Buying a home is a liability. I know people will read this and say, "How is my home a liability, everyone says it's an asset" and I can understand why you might be saying or thinking this. An asset by definition is something that feeds your pocket (Goose translation) and a liability eats your pocket. So look at your home, is it paying you every month to live there? Most of us will answer this with a no, our home isn't paying us to live there, we are actually paying for it. Correct! But Goose, aren't I building equity by owning a home versus just renting? And again, I can understand this thought process very well because I thought the same thing. Your home is a liability until the day you sell it, or rent it. Your home is a forced savings account at best. This is how we look at our primary home. It's just a forced savings account. If you rented out your home as an Airbnb or something like that, then it could be an asset because it is feeding your pocket; it's paying you every month. However, every day it's not rented it costs you money.

We bought the duplex for $175,000 with an FHA Loan. This allowed us to only have to put 3.5% down. Buying our duplex added about $200 extra to our monthly payment. Now this is one reason we love real estate so much. In real estate, $1 will get you $4-$5 worth of real estate. HUH? What do you mean? Normally you are required to put 20% to 30% down for a piece of real estate. It's your down payment. (Yes, you can get away with putting less down but you will also have to pay PMI which is Property Mortgage Insurance. After the 2008 housing crash, banks and lenders came up with this PMI so people could still buy homes.)

So If you had $50,000 you could buy $200,000 worth of real estate. If you had $100,000 you could buy $500,000 worth of real estate. Can you follow the math? $1 gets you $4-$5 worth of real estate; it just depends on what type of loan you get, and this is how you use LEVERAGE. You can leverage your $1 to get $4. It's an amazing tool to know how to use. The banks love giving you money for great assets. Remember, assets feed your pocket, not eat your pocket.

It's interesting to me that a bank will lend you 75%-80% of the cost of a piece of real estate and yet they won't lend you money so you can go buy that bank's company stock. Think about that. Why would the bank give you money for real estate and not their own stock? If a bank won't lend on it, then why would you buy it? More on this later in the Assets chapter.

So we were able to buy our $175,000 duplex for only $6,125...WHAT? We were able to trade our $6,125 for a cash flowing asset worth $175,000 plus the income it produced! How is that even possible? If it's that easy, why doesn't everyone just do that? Because you aren't taught how to become wealthy. The cards aren't in your favor because it's all a game. So you have to learn the rules of the game.

It's easier to learn the rules of the rich than to try to change them. Wealthy people use leverage and credit responsibly to purchase assets that pay them every month. One reason that I am writing this book is that I wish I had had someone to explain these principles to me. I would have been able to get ahead so much faster had I known what I am teaching you now.

Don't dwell on what you didn't know. Instead, take these God Money Empire secrets and apply them, as I did, in your life and you, too, will become wealthy. Money is a game; learn the rules of the game and build your God Money Empire!

5 THE GOD MONEY 10% 20% 70% FRAMEWORK

Ecclesiastes 11:1-6

1 Ship your grain across the sea;

   after many days you may receive a return.

2 Invest in seven ventures, yes, in eight;

   you do not know what disaster may come upon the land.

3 If clouds are full of water,

   they pour rain on the earth.

Whether a tree falls to the south or to the north,

   in the place where it falls, there it will lie.

4 Whoever watches the wind will not plant;

   whoever looks at the clouds will not reap.

5 As you do not know the path of the wind,

   or how the body is formed[a] in a mother's womb,

so you cannot understand the work of God,

   the Maker of all things.

6 Sow your seed in the morning,

   and at evening let your hands not be idle,

for you do not know which will succeed,

   whether this or that,

   or whether both will do equally well.

This is a very powerful yet practical chapter. The God Money 10%20%70% Rule is a secret playbook on what to do with every dollar you earn, how to multiply it and never be broke again! If you do only this one thing out of this whole book, you would absolutely be able to build your God Money Empire.

The God Money 10%20%70% Rule is broken down into three parts. The first part is the 10%. For every dollar you earn, 10%, or $0.10, is going to be tithed; it's going to your church. You want God in your finances. If you are obedient in tithing, He can accelerate your abundant living and finances. Tithing is a heart position. You don't tithe in order to get; however, God is so good and gracious that He will bless your obedience and your tithes.

The next part is 20%. For every dollar you earn, 20%, or $0.20, is going to be put in a Save to Invest account, maybe in a savings account at your local bank. This money isn't to be saved, it's to be invested later. This is a huge mindset shift that needs to happen. Money is a tool and it is only good when it's being used. Money just sitting in the bank isn't being allowed to grow or do what it was created to do.

The third part is 70%. For every dollar you earn, 70%, or $0.70, is going to be used to live off. This is what you get to use for your bills, your fun money, etc. If 70% isn't enough to live off, then you need to do one of two things… preferably both. You need to increase your income so that the 70% can cover your current living expenses, or you need to reduce your living expenses for now. If you did both of these things you would be able to master the God Money 10%20%70% Rule and move on to the 10%40%50% Rule. More on this later.

I started doing this when I was selling RVs and making $49,000 for my first year. The rough numbers for that broke down like this:

Earned Income: $49,000

10%-----------------$4,900

20%-----------------$9,800

70%-----------------$34,300

I was renting a house with roommates at the time and doing my best to not spend any money outside of my absolute needs. This way I was able to actually take money from my 70% account and move it to my 20% Save to Invest account–not every month, but in the months when I had leftover money. Using my example, if my lifestyle didn't change and my income didn't change, in 20 years I would have earned $1,000,000, have tithed to my church $100,000 and have saved $200,000 to invest. Now, I am not recommending you do this, because you can build wealth more quickly if you invest along the way and if you focus on increasing your income. I will walk you through this and share exactly how I did it. The goal here is learning this new discipline and being okay with temporarily giving leisure a back seat. If you can punt leisure now, you can have luxury later!

Why Tithe 10%?

The word *tithe* in Hebrew literally means "tenth." We are called to tithe 10% of our earnings. Tithing is a special gift from God. Wait, how is it a gift from God when it's my money I'm giving to God? God, the creator of all, doesn't need your tithe; however, you need to give your tithe so that God can bless you with abundance. Your tithe is an invitation to God. When you tithe you are telling God there is nothing I have that You can't have. When God knows He can trust you with a little, He will bless you with much. It's interesting how God says to test Him in this. He is talking about tithing. When we are obedient and tithe, God opens doors that were closed, He shows you opportunities that weren't there, and He showers you with blessings and joy. We can't outgive God. He is an abundant God who wants to bless His children.

Tithing has been a huge part of my testimony and a huge part of why I have been so successful. Chances are we don't go to the same church, and no, your pastor didn't pay me to tell you to tithe. When you understand that God is a gracious and loving God who wants to bless you, and that the way to allow Him to do that is by your obedience in tithing, then you will look forward to tithing. You will adopt the heart of a cheerful giver. That's what God is after–not your wallet or bank account, but your heart.

Why 20% Save to Invest?

At first it is going to be difficult feeling like you are building your God Money Empire by only saving to invest 20% of your income. This is where you have to just trust the process and allow God the opportunity to do His part. It might seem odd to read that last sentence because God *always* does His part. You are the one that has to do *your* part. And that means tithing 10% and saving to invest 20% of your income.

Dr. Dharius Daniels, lead pastor of Change Church says, "Sometimes God's plan is God's preferences," meaning God loves you enough to have this amazing life for you but He respects you enough to allow you to make your own choices. So just because God wants something for your life doesn't mean it will happen. You also have to want the same thing. Your will be done, not mine. Your obedience is what allows you to be able to step into His amazing and abundant life. The 20% is going to take time to grow. It is going to take faith in the process. One day you will find that your Save to Invest account has enough money to allow you to purchase a cash flowing asset, and that will start to feel like you are finally building your God Money Empire. I love what Tony Robbins says: "We overestimate what we can do in a year and underestimate what we can do in a decade." Faith, patience, and a plan are how you build wealth. Being able to save 20% to invest is a critical piece to the God Money wealth building formula.

Ecclesiastes 11:1-6 shows us we need more than one stream of income, more than one investment, more than one asset. It's interesting how so many millionaires talk about having seven or eight streams of income. Hmm… wonder where that principle came from. Hint, hint…Ecclesiastes 11:1-6. With your 20% you will be able to buy income. When you buy an asset, that cash flows monthly—in other words, you are literally buying income. So the duplex we bought for $175,000 and only put $6,125 down was how we were able to build wealth and buy another stream of income. The rents at the time were around $850 each side. So every month it was making us an additional $1,700, which is an extra $20,400 gross income for the year. That's a pretty good ROI (return on investment). I will help you be able to make more sense of this in a later chapter.

Why 70% to live off of?

The way I was able to accelerate my wealth building was by following my God Money 10%20%70% Rule.

This was based on a $50,000 annual income. Now I was single at the time with no kids. So for you, you might need to adjust these numbers and percentages a little but 10%20%70% should be your first goal.

If you are committed to building your God Money Empire you might need to adjust your current lifestyle and expenses. If you don't think you can tithe 10%, save to invest 20%, and live off 70% then you need to either cut your expenses or increase your income. More on this in the next chapter. It takes discipline and faith to stick with the 10%20%70% Rule. If you are making $100,000 or even $250,000 I would keep your living expenses as close to 70% of $50,000 as possible. This is what I did and after I got married, my wife was on board. We knew if we could just stay disciplined and pay the price now, then we would be able to pay any price later. I think it's important to note that you will only be living this way for a little while. That could be two years, five years or twenty years, but what kind of life will you be able to live if you just stick to this plan long enough to reap the rewards? How many people could you bless? What kind of house could you live in or cars would you have? How many vacations could you take? Could you retire ten or twenty years earlier if you just decided to commit to the God Money 10%20%70% Rule? I have already done the hard part for you to see if this works and we have proven it does; you get to copy this blueprint and hopefully hit your goals and targets sooner than we did. Make the decision and go after the abundant life God has for you!

This one simple God Money Framework has the potential to mean you will never be broke again. Wealth building takes sacrifice and discipline. Anything worth having does. This framework is how you build wealth and create financial freedom. If you don't get anything else from this book, just know that God will bless your 10% tithe one way or another. God will open doors for you to invest your 20% STI Account if you're seeking His wisdom. God will allow 70% to stretch further than you think if you have faith for that. Being wealthy has more to do with your heart and the biblical principles in which you steward what God has blessed you with. All of this takes faith and acting like God is telling the truth. You can do this. Just use the tools and frameworks in this book long enough to see the results you want. If He did it for me, He will do it for you. He has great plans for you.

6 INCREASE YOUR INCOME

COLOSSIANS 3:23

Whatever you do, whatever kind of work you are doing, work heartily, with all your heart and all the different ways that play out in scripture, with Christ-like character, with honesty, with diligence, with integrity, with humility. So work heartily as for the Lord and not for men.

I love this scripture! It almost has a Braveheart feel to it. We all have more in us. We all can do more because we can all become more, and if we can become more we can do more and have more!

Like everything else, Christianity has extremes. There are pastors and churches that focus and preach prosperity gospel, which is different from prosperity *in* the gospel. There are also pastors and churches that preach the opposite and focus on asking God for nothing and wanting nothing, thinking they are holier for doing so. You aren't being holy; rather, you're being a burden to those around you because of your lack of money, and your unwillingness to figure out how to get more of it makes you part of the problem instead of the solution. If God is as big as we say He is, or better yet, if God is as big as *He* says He is, why couldn't you ask Him for anything? Why couldn't you ask for nicer things? Why couldn't you ask to have a Lamborghini or Ferrari or Gulfstream G650? He already gave us the perfect gift... Jesus! So anything else that we ask for is not only easy for God but it allows God to be the generous God that He is. He is a great Father. Great fathers know what their children want and need and they want to bless their children.

God doesn't care about you having things, He just doesn't want the things to have you! Bishop T.D. Jakes once said, "I don't want anything that God doesn't want for me, but I do want EVERYTHING God wants for me." What a great point. Why wouldn't it be okay to ask God for everything that He wants for you? This is where you need to spend time in prayer, asking God: What do You have in store for me? For my family? For my purpose? For my job? For my business? For my community? Have the willingness to be used by God and He will bless your stinkin' socks off! Why would He do this? Because He's God!

Now that we can wrap our minds around the fact that God *wants* to bless us and He *will* bless us, let's figure out what we can do to walk in His blessings and favor. God has already blessed you with everything you need to take your next steps. He has given you certain talents and abilities that He can use if you'll let Him. God will take you places your character alone can't take you. When you are walking faithfully with God, He will open doors and reveal new opportunities. It doesn't matter whether you have a job or own a business, you need to be thinking about how you can increase your income.

Most of my adult life I have been in sales. I was working for a company, getting paid to sell their products. When I was a waiter at our local Brazilian restaurant, I was selling their food and an experience. When I was selling RVs, I was trying to get as many families as possible their own Memory Machines—that's what I would call the RVs so they could go camping and make those special memories with family and friends. When I was selling HVAC units I tried to solve as many problems as possible and focused on making the contractors I was working with more profitable. We currently own four businesses and are constantly looking for ways to increase our income. Why? Because God created us for more and we want EVERYTHING God has in store for us. God doesn't necessarily give you wealth; He gives you the ability to produce wealth. Deuteronomy 8:17-18. We want to be good stewards of what He has blessed us with and part of that, I believe, is growing, not just managing, what He's given us. When we produce more we can give more, bless more, and care for more. Recognizing everything good comes from God, we are to make sure our hearts are God focused and not blessing focused.

If you have a job, you need to go to your manager, supervisor, or boss and ask what you need to do to get a pay raise. As an employer my ears start singing when I hear a team member of mine ask if there is anything they can take off my plate or if there is any skill they can learn to add value to our company. Open communication with your boss is how you can very clearly and easily increase your income. Even if it isn't right away, there is a lot of trust earned when you have the courage to have these kinds of conversations with your team leader and you have a clear path to your next raise. The truth is, the company you work for can pay you more; you just need to figure out how they can make sense of it.

If you are a front desk person or in an administrative position, it might seem like an entry level position with entry level pay. Ask the question and think about what else is needed here? What can I be doing to create more value or find the company new money? Businesses get to pay more and grow when there is an increase in sales. It's the new money all businesses are looking for. A new client or customer. A new product, or processes that can save the business money. As an employee you should be constantly looking for ways to make the company you work for healthier and more money. Then *you* can become more valuable to that company and earn more money yourself. Most good employers are looking for their core team, for the people who want to grow the business and are invested in the mission. These people are the ones who get rewarded and paid the most. As you keep learning new skills, become so valuable that your company has to pay you more. Otherwise, someone else will notice how great you are and will offer you a better opportunity. But before you go looking for something better, look within the company you are currently working for and, as long as you agree with the mission and like what you're doing, see how you can get promoted within that company first. If they aren't willing to make sense of the investment in you, *then* you can start looking for better opportunities.

One thing I've always told people who have decided to move on from our team is that I understand you have to do what's best for you and your family. Yes, I want to keep great people, but I also want employees to find their God-given purpose, and if that's on my team, then great. If it's not, then I hope that what they learned from our companies would stick with them and help get them a better opportunity for their future.

I once had a young guy who worked for one of our Medical Supply companies give me his two week notice because he said he just wasn't passionate about braces anymore. As we were having this heart to heart I looked at him and said, "Do you think I'm passionate about braces?" His face looked very confused and he finally said, "Well, yes, it's your company." Then I told him, "I'm passionate about people, not braces. I love people. I don't care what job or business I have as long as it's giving me the opportunity to help and love on people. Then I know I'm walking in my purpose. This will look a little different for each of us but that is why it is so important to be praying and walking with God through the process. Pray bold prayers and have high expectations and God will provide. If it's God guided it will be God provided.

In everything you do, do it for the Lord and not for man. Never stop learning and continue to skill stack.

SKILL STACKING

Skill stacking is when you learn a skill: let's say it's washing windows. Then you can take that skill and learn how to market your ability to wash windows.

Now you can wash windows *and* get new business. Now you can learn how to streamline your process and make it duplicable. Now you can wash windows, market your skill, do it efficiently and learn how to hire great team members to help. Now you have a company that can scale because you just took one skill and kept learning and stacking until you had a business. You can do this with anything.

In your current job, what additional skill could you learn each year? each quarter? each month? How much more valuable could you become to your company so they would have to pay you more? Think of what others need and reverse engineer that into a skill or service. The bigger the problem you can solve, the bigger the money you will earn. People need solutions, not more problems. Focus on the solution and you'll increase your income faster than anyone else that is focused on only doing the one thing they were hired to do.

BE-DO-HAVE

I learned this concept of BE-DO-HAVE from Myron Golden, who was a pastor and now is an amazing Christian businessman and coach. The core concept of BE-DO-HAVE is this:

BE little

DO little

HAVE little

If you become little, you'll do little, and if you do little you'll have little.

BE more

DO more

HAVE more

If you become more, you can do more, and you'll have more.

Myron Golden also says the thing that will keep someone from making $1,000,000 a year is making $500,000 a year. We get comfortable and settle. This is why I'm more interested in my potential and who God created me to be than making a certain dollar amount. Yes, goals and targets are important, but who you become is more important than the amount of money you make. So the person who is making $50,000 a year and really should only be making $20,000, you are a rockstar and an inspiration. If you are the person making $50,000 a year who settled and should be making $500,000, you need to stop being so selfish. You need to focus more on your purpose and others rather than the $50,000 lifestyle you've gotten comfortable with that doesn't allow you to look beyond your own needs.

It's a very simple concept, but one that needs meditation and prayer. This goes back to the importance of your God Money Mindset we talked about earlier. Think about this for a moment: when the almighty God created you perfectly in your mother's womb, do you think God's purpose and desire for you was to become less than He created you to be, or ALL He created you to be? Do you think God wants good for your life or the best for your life? With all the amazing things God created, wouldn't it make sense that He also created an amazing life filled with abundance for you and not just a life of mediocrity? I believe every day I get to wake up is an opportunity to discover more of God's blessings for my life. I wake up expecting to be amazed by God because He is amazing.

I don't watch the news, I don't spend time with negative people, I just focus on God's abundance. That's why I constantly look for increase and what I need to be doing to increase what God has given me. You see, God is so good, He will let us settle at whatever level we decide to settle. But you have people counting on you more than you know. *They* need you to increase your income more than *you* need you to increase your income. I don't want to just make it to heaven; I want the most out of my life. Don't settle on good, go for God's best!

7 ASSET ACCUMULATION & HOUSE HACKING

MATTHEW 25:14-30

The Parable of the Bags of Gold

14 "Again, it will be like a man going on a journey, who called his servants and entrusted his wealth to them. 15 To one he gave five bags of gold, to another two bags, and to another one bag,[a] each according to his ability. Then he went on his journey. 16 The man who had received five bags of gold went at once and put his money to work and gained five bags more. 17 So also, the one with two bags of gold gained two more. 18 But the man who had received one bag went off, dug a hole in the ground and hid his master's money. 19 After a long time the master of those servants returned and settled accounts with them. 20 The man who had received five bags of gold brought the other five. 'Master,' he said, 'you entrusted me with five bags of gold. See, I have gained five more.'
21 His master replied, 'Well done, good and faithful servant! You have been faithful with a few things; I

will put you in charge of many things. Come and share your master's happiness!'

22 The man with two bags of gold also came. 'Master,' he said, 'you entrusted me with two bags of gold; see, I have gained two more.'

23 His master replied, 'Well done, good and faithful servant! You have been faithful with a few things; I will put you in charge of many things. Come and share your master's happiness!'

24 Then the man who had received one bag of gold came. 'Master,' he said, 'I knew that you are a hard man, harvesting where you have not sown and gathering where you have not scattered seed. 25 So I was afraid and went out and hid your gold in the ground. See, here is what belongs to you.'

26 His master replied, 'You wicked, lazy servant! So you knew that I harvest where I have not sown and gather where I have not scattered seed? 27 Well then, you should have put my money on deposit with the bankers, so that when I returned I would have received it back with interest.

28 "So take the bag of gold from him and give it to the one who has ten bags. 29 For whoever has will be given more, and they will have an abundance. Whoever does not have, even what they have will be taken from them. 30 And throw that worthless servant outside, into the darkness, where there will be weeping and gnashing of teeth.'"

I love this parable. There is a lot in it. It shows us that we are supposed to use what God has blessed us with. When we do so, we are blessed even more-- from having courage, taking risks, and having a growth mentality, a God Money Mindset. These are all things we must become more comfortable with in order to further the Kingdom.

The parable talks about how two of the three servants were faithful stewards of what they were given to manage. On the other hand, the one who decided to take the easy way and settle was punished for doing so.

It's interesting how the one who had five bags of gold that he turned into ten and the one who had two bags of gold that he turned into four, were praised equally by their master. It's because throughout the Bible money is looked at in percentages and not amounts. This is a crucial point and worth underlining and never forgetting. God views money in percentages, not amounts; we should do the same. When you can begin to look at money in percentages rather than amounts, then you will be able to use and view money like God does--in percentages.

MONEY IN PERCENTAGES VS. AMOUNTS

God asks us to give as we have been given. The word "as" isn't saying an amount, it's representing a percentage in which you've been blessed–in other words, in the same measure. Oftentimes we can make sense of things that are cheaper in price, rather than things that are better in quality but cost more, because we are focused on the amount and not the percentage those things represent according to our wealth.

For example, my wife really wanted a Louis Vuitton handbag. Now my wife isn't materialistic at all. She rarely asks for things, and to my knowledge this was the first time I had heard her even talk about wanting a designer bag. The bag was around $4,000. She kept looking at it and running numbers on it, trying to make sense of how she could talk herself and myself into actually buying one. Now if this was when we were newly married there wouldn't even have been a conversation because we were broke. We were making around $100k a year and lived in half of a duplex that we owned. Now to most, this wouldn't look like we were broke at all... in fact, making six figures and already having multiple properties is more than most people will ever accumulate in their lifetime. This has more to do with your goals and standards than it does with your reality.

We were broke based on our goals and standards. Broke based on what we were wanting and trying to build, not what we were wanting to spend. We were okay with postponing leisure for a later time in life. We chose to stay disciplined in our GOD MONEY 10%20%70% Framework so we could build our wealth and not just buy things. Please pause and think about that for a second... The goals and dreams you have, the things you are trying to accomplish—how much are you sacrificing your future so that your current self can have a luxurious lifestyle? Now I say "luxurious" loosely because if you are choosing to spend all your money on things and not willing to tithe or pay yourself or even put money away so you can invest it later, then you are living above your means and you will never be able to build wealth. The comforts you are accumulating now are stealing from the assets your family could enjoy later. If you can just decide to be disciplined now and apply the principles in this book, you will be able to become wealthy. I know this to be true because this is how I did it. Now back to my wife's Louis bag!

Seven years later, and after achieving millionaire status, is when she started actually thinking about buying a $4,000 bag. If you do things in order you can have anything you want. Goose, what do you mean by that? I mean if you can focus on getting your money right and get to a point where you aren't going broke to have nice things, then you can spend money on whatever you want. Let your assets pay for your liabilities.

Kelsie was running the numbers, but rather than focusing on the amount of a $4,000 handbag, she compared it to our net worth at the time. That $4,000 Louis Vuitton handbag made up about 0.1% of our net worth. So it was going to cost me 0.1% of our net worth. That looks and feels very different from spending $4,000 on a handbag. This helped put things into perspective for us both. Deep down I wanted to buy her the bag and anything else she wanted. Why wouldn't I? She is the mother of my children and my amazing wife!

Being able to get on the same page financially with her and work towards similar goals has allowed us to stay disciplined and be able to spend $4,000 on a handbag for my wife and not even feel it.

I don't say this is a bragging way at all; I say it as inspiration and also to let you know it's okay to want the Louis Vuitton bags and the Rolls Royces and the Gulfstream Jet. The important thing is to do these things in order so you don't become broke trying to buy the things you want. So many people go broke trying to look rich. God has no problem with you having things, He just doesn't want things to have you! He is the provider and the source of all great things. Learn to love the Giver and not the gifts.

Now look at it from this perspective. If someone buys a car for $20,000, it makes sense because that is a "normal" amount to pay for a car. Please understand I am generalizing and assuming here. But if someone is driving around a Lamborghini Urus that costs $250,000 we say that's such a waste of money, or why would you spend so much on a car? It's ridiculous. Now the person who bought the $20k car makes $40k a year. Is it still smart for that person to buy a $20k car? The person driving the $250k car makes $500K a year. Is it still ridiculous that a person is driving around that car? Now take emotions out of it and look at percentages. Both of these people spend 50% of their yearly income on a car. I would say both scenarios are ridiculous but they spent the same percentage of money that they each had. Spending 50% of your yearly income for a car that's a liability is a waste of money in my opinion. However, if you are able to write your car off or use it to help you earn more money, then that might be worth the money spent.

This is why the God Money 10%20%70% Framework and 10%40%50% Framework are so important, because it is based on a percentage and not amounts.

When you can be obedient in your tithes and offerings and view money like God does, then you have positioned yourself to be blessed financially.

Let's look at the God Money 10%20%70% Framework and what we already learned so far. The 20% was to be placed in an STI account or a "Save To Invest" account. So once you have enough money to invest in a monthly cash flowing asset, then you spend that money. This is how you get your money to work for you.

This is what we did. At the time my wife and I were newly married and I brought my newly-learned discipline of 10%20%70% into our marriage. She was on board and so together we were able to stick to this plan and duplicate our efforts. Were we perfect? Absolutely not. But we were moving in the right direction and developing the investor muscles. We had enough money put away to invest in some real estate. We decided to buy a duplex.

Here are the numbers on that duplex: asking price was $175,000 and the rents were about $750 and $850. We had an FHA loan which at the time had a downpayment requirement of 3.5% of the asking price. So for that duplex, we were able to buy two addresses for 3.5% of $175,000 or $6,125. This is one of the things I love about real estate and the power of leverage. We were able to buy a $175,000 asset for $6,125. Most people would say we paid $175,000 for it but the truth is we only paid the down payment. Only if you pay cash for something do you ever pay the actual asking price of that property.

This duplex was the first real asset we purchased and it would be one of the best investments we had ever made. From this purchase we were able to buy another house about six months after moving into the duplex. We asked our lender if there was any way we could buy another property. Well, there is always a way to do something and to get something done. This is another interesting point to make: almost every property or business we have ever bought, we didn't even have the money for the purchase at the time, but we were determined to find a way. "With the faith of a mustard seed you can move a mountain." Our lender informed us of a strategy where we could get qualified to purchase another home with a different type of home loan. So we went with a 5% down loan and were able to purchase another property. That's three properties in under a year. This is how we were able to do that.

For the duplex, I was making 100% commission at my job selling RVs . When you're in sales you typically have to have at least two years of proven income before getting qualified to purchase a home. Shortly after buying the duplex I switched jobs to selling commercial HVAC systems and my payplan changed to a salary plus bonuses. This was interesting to me because I had only had the new job for about two or three weeks when we started to get qualified to purchase another home. The fact that I was on salary at my new job didn't matter. I was able to get qualified for another home loan.

The new job was paying $70,000 base salary plus potential bonuses; the new home we wanted was $168,000. Let's back up for a second. The reason we were able to only put 3.5% down on the duplex was that it was our primary residence. We converted the duplex into a rental and bought the new house for $168,000. This was now our primary residence. So we were able to count the rental income we were making from the duplex to help us qualify to buy the new home. Pretty cool, huh?! So with this new home being $168,000 we had to put down 5% of the asking price. This ended up being around $8,400. How much did we buy this new home for? $168,000? Nope... We bought that $168,000 asset for only $8,400. We don't really count our mortgage as the cost of the home because you have to live somewhere and we look at the mortgage as a forced savings account for a later date. So a $6,125 duplex down payment plus an $8,400 new house down payment totaled $14,525 of actual out-of-pocket money to purchase three properties equaling $343,000 worth of real estate in less than eight months, also adding $22,800 of rental income to my $70,000 salary job. That's a gross income of $92,800 just by putting my money to work.

STAY BROKE:

Grant Cardone has this rule of "staying broke" and what he means by this is to stack your money and then dump it into a monthly cash flowing asset like real estate. Go broke on the asset. You aren't really going broke. However, you are taking your STI (Save to Invest) money and spending all of that on the asset. Getting that STI account down to zero then forces you to rebuild your 20% STI account so you can "Go Broke" again on the next asset. This is the simple strategy we use with our 20% STI account to build wealth and repeat.

I was soon promoted with my HVAC sales job, meaning a move to California. After praying and talking it over with my wife, we decided it would be good for us to take on this opportunity. We knew no one where we were moving to but that was exciting, to get the chance to create a new life together.

We would be leaving our comfy 3 bed 2 bath home with a yard by the park and moving into a 2 bed 1 bath 800 sq. ft. apartment with a tiny concrete pad in Walnut Creek, CA. The apartment was nice enough, but tight. Once again we were deciding to postpone leisure now so our future selves could have something better for our family. We were able to turn our home we left in Idaho into our third rental. Our duplex was paying us $1,900 a month and our home was now paying us $1,250. So a gross grand total of $3,150 a month and $37,800 a year.

Our new rent in our little apartment was $2,500 a month, I believe, which was almost the same price as all of our rental mortgages combined. My new job was paying me a salary of $125,000 plus bonuses and we were still sticking to the 10%20%70% GOD MONEY Framework. We were living and acting like we were still broke because we were on a mission to build wealth. We had no kids yet and just focused on making as much as we could with the skills that we had. Sacrifice and discipline are required to build something great. We are now in a position where we have more options than obligations because of these little steps we took early on.

One random August lunch break in Concord, CA I felt a Holy Spirit impression to call my old landlord, Craig, in Boise, ID. It just so happened to be his birthday and I told him we wanted to buy his apartment complex. Years ago, when I was younger and had a credit score of 407 but was trying to get my life on track, Craig and his wife Danna were so kind and took a chance on me, renting me one of the units. Before that, everyone who ran my credit would just ghost me and so I was having a hard time finding a place to rent. I didn't blame them, though, because I wouldn't want to rent to me, either. Finally I found this little apartment on Craigslist and asked if the landlords would show me the unit. I thought if they got to meet me in person they would see who I was and know that I wasn't some sketchy dude but I was just a dude with a bad credit score. They met me, were very kind and gave me a chance. To this day I am forever grateful for them. I had the thought that one day I would buy this apartment complex from them. So that was always in my mind and I shared that with my wife. Back to the call with Craig.

It was his birthday so I told him happy birthday and that my reason for calling was to let him know we wanted to buy his apartment complex... Now we had money in our STI account but not nearly enough to buy this apartment complex. However, I knew God wanted me to call him that day so I did. I let Craig know my intentions for the call and how we wanted to buy the complex from him. There was some small talk and then he said that they weren't going to sell the complex at this time; however, they did have a business that they might be ready to sell. I said "Great, please send me the numbers and we will take a look." OK, honesty time: I had zero intentions of buying his business from him. I wanted his real estate. However, God had other plans. This is why prayer and asking God for wisdom and for things is important. He wants to be part of your plan because if you're willing to partner up with God, He will bless you far greater than your own plans.

Craig gave me a brief run-down on why they were selling and what the business was. He then sent us over the P&L (Profit & Loss) report and Balance sheet. Now I had no idea what a P&L or balance sheet even was but I told Craig I was excited to review them later that night with my wife. A profit and loss report shows the company's revenues and expenses during a particular period. It indicates how the revenues are transformed into the net income or net profit. A balance sheet is a summary of the financial balances of an individual or organization, whether it be a sole proprietorship, a business partnership, a corporation, private limited company or other organization such as a government or not-for-profit entity.

Later that night we were reviewing the P&L and Balance Sheet and noticed that this medical bracing company actually made money. I looked at the bottom of the P&L Sheet and saw a positive number. In my mind I thought, *so we can mess this up a little bit and still make money*. My simple mind concluded that this was a profitable business that just needed some new life blood to drive up sales and make it become a better, more efficiently run business. We could earn while we learned. We prayed about it and decided to see if we could even buy this business. At this point we were expecting our first child. We knew we wanted to move back to Idaho to raise our family. My old HVAC job had been taken over by someone else so there wouldn't be a job for me to go back to. So I knew if we couldn't buy this business I would go back to selling RVs. Fast forward: after praying together about it, we had peace and agreed on the price of the medical supply business.

The price for the business was $500,000 plus the inventory. We were working with several different banks and not really getting anywhere with them. Most of them either said we didn't have any experience in that industry or there was too much Blue Sky Effect attached with the business. Blue Sky Effect means there aren't enough tangible assets to the business. Your business is more valuable because of the "book of business" (repeat customers) and not necessarily because of the assets associated with the company. We knew even though we kept getting No's that God had a YES for us. We didn't know how we were actually going to pull this off, but we still had peace that it was going to happen. This conversation started in August 2017 and it was now October 2017 and our baby girl, Ella Grace, was born. Two weeks after her birth I put in my two-week notice at my HVAC sales job; two weeks after that we decided to move back to Idaho and live in our little cozy home again. Ella was just four weeks old and Kelsie was still recovering from having Ella when we loaded up everything we had with help from friends and my amazing in-laws and moved back to Idaho. I'm now jobless, we are living off our STI account and have a month-old baby. It's crazy reliving this because I remember having so much faith in what God was going to do for our family yet not having much faith in what *I* was going to do for my family.

It took six months to negotiate this business deal

and I had the same bank tell me NO eight times... However, I already knew God had said Yes, so I was determined to figure out the how. We went to visit my in-laws in Denver for the holidays and just hung out there for a while, continuing to drain our STI account. Kelsie and I were talking one day about what we were going to do if we weren't able to buy the business and I assured her everything was going to be just fine; if this deal didn't happen then I was going to be selling RVs again. That day or a couple days later we prayed a bold prayer and got specific with God. We said "God, if it's your will for us to buy this business, then give us a YES by Friday morning; if not, we are going to turn the page...Amen." This was a Monday or Tuesday and on that Thursday morning we got a call from the same bank that had told us NO eight times over the course of six months. Congratulations, we were approved and the business was going to be ours! We were over the moon excited and couldn't believe what had just happened. It's amazing how God will bless you if you just let Him. Let Him be a part of your goals and your plans. God has an amazing life for you! Sometimes you can see what the next steps are and sometimes you can't. You have to just keep walking in faith. One of the craziest things about this story is that we bought this multimillion-dollar medical company with zero money out of pocket… That's right, $0! Remember the little duplex we bought? We were able to put a second lien on that property as collateral for our new business loan. The value of equity we thought we had was $50,000. That equity ended up being our down payment for the business. We didn't even have to get the bank that $50,000; they just let us use the equity. So from that $6,125, or 3.5%, duplex down payment we were not only able to buy a duplex but also a multimillion-dollar medical company. You don't need to know exactly how to do something, you just need to trust God in the process and take the next steps. We knew God had this business for us, we just didn't know how. We stayed faithful and persistent and God blessed that.

I often think about what would have happened if we had given up after the first NO from the bank... or the second or third or fourth or fifth.... How different our lives would be and how different our team's lives would be. Your decisions and determination don't just affect you; they affect everyone around you. So when you hear God say YES, know that He means YES. You just need to be obedient and do your part. As the Bible says, "Faith without works is dead." Keep working on your God Money Mindset and be clear with what you ask God.

My favorite asset classes are Real Estate and Businesses. They have far superior returns, tremendous appreciation, and unbeatable tax advantages. Buying assets such as these are how the rich don't pay taxes...legally! One of our tax saving strategies is to buy at least one piece of real estate each year to legally avoid paying taxes. Not all assets are created equally. Stocks and bonds are known by the majority as assets, but I would argue that if that's true they are the worst kind of assets to own. There is zero forced appreciation and to my knowledge zero tax advantage. Think of it this way: if you go into a bank and ask the bank for a loan to buy that bank's stock, you will get denied. Now you go to the same bank and ask for a loan on a fourplex, they will gladly lend you the money for that real estate. Isn't that interesting? The bank knows their money is safer in real estate than in the casino... I mean the stock market. Some people have done very well with stocks and bonds. However, real estate is a much simpler strategy to understand plus you have more control over it. Real estate is all about timing, while the stock market is truly a gamble. Warren Buffett's three rules to investing are: 1. Never lose money 2. Never lose money 3. Never lose money. He might seem like a guy who won at stocks; however, he owns whole companies, not just the stocks. More millionaires are created with real estate than any other industry. It does take time to learn but it's a game worth learning.

KNOW YOUR EXIT:

I'm sure you've heard the saying: You make money when you buy the deal, not sell the deal. This statement is referring to making sure you have a great deal from day one and not just praying that one day it will all pan out for you. Going into a deal, I'm looking for a handful of things. Can I add value? Can I bump up rents to market value? How do I exit this deal?

I love value-added properties and we have done very well with them. A value-added property is a place that just needs some TLC. You could do a big remodel or you could just clean and paint. I like these properties because I know I can make it force appreciate. What does that mean? I can put some sweat equity into the property and make it worth more than I bought it for.

Ninety percent of the properties we have bought have been in this value add category and it's been one of the reasons we have never lost money on a deal. If rents are below market value and the property needs some TLC, this is a big score! Remember that duplex on which we put $6,125 down? We added about $10,000 worth of rehab (new floors, carpets, paint, fireplace surround, and backsplash) and held it for about four years. The purchase price was $175,000. Four years later we sold that duplex for $315,000. So that duplex paid us an average of $2,000 a month which is $24,000 a year plus it appreciated $35,000 for four years. For our little down payment of $6,125 plus $10,000 worth of upgrades with an all-in cost of $16,125, we made an ROI (Return on Investment) of $236,000. Not to mention all the tax advantages we were able to get. We decided to sell this duplex but we could have done a cash out refinance and kept the duplex and taken out 80% of the value of the property. We took the profit, rolled it into a 1031 Exchange and bought three more properties. A 1031 Exchange is basically an account that your money goes into that you can't touch until you buy more like kind real estate. You use a 1031 Exchange to legally get out of paying taxes. This is a tool the rich use to get richer. So when you are looking at a deal, know how you're going to get out of that deal before you buy it. Having a couple different exit strategies will minimize your risk and will give you a better understanding on when you are going to sell or refinance. Developing these skills and knowing what the rich are looking for in a real estate deal will allow you to build wealth and be a good steward of what God has blessed you with so you can also bless others.

Be like the servants who pleased God. Look at the blessings you already have and figure out a way to multiply them. Turn your 1 into 2 and your 5 into 10. Accumulating assets and becoming wealthy should be more about becoming who God created you to be than the things you accumulate. Use your talents, use your resources and focus on your God-given purpose to be able to create the abundant life He has in store for you. This does look different for everyone but what God has for you is special for you. He designed life that way so everyone could walk in His blessings and favor. God has no problem with you having stuff; He just doesn't want stuff to have you.

8 INCREASE YOUR INCOME "AGAIN"

Deuteronomy 8:18

But remember the LORD your God, for it is he who gives you the ability to produce wealth, and so confirms his covenant, which he swore to your forefathers, as it is today.

LUKE 16:10

Whoever can be trusted with very little can also be trusted with much, and whoever is dishonest with very little will also be dishonest with much.

Congratulations! By now you are deep in the God Money Framework! You now know what it takes to have a God Money Mindset. You understand that money is just a tool and meant to be used. You understand the importance of tithing and how God will bless your tithes one way or another. You know how to use leverage and the importance of having a good credit score. You are using the 10%20%70%

God Money Framework and have a STI Account. You have been able to revisit your job or business and increase your income by utilizing the proven God Money Strategies provided in this book, and learned the importance of asset accumulation and house hacking as a way of building up your wealth. It's now time to….. Yup! Increase Your Income, again!

This isn't a repeat chapter; it's just that important! You need to be focused on finding creative ways to use everything God has given you to increase your income so you can do more kingdom work. The more you have, the more you can do. The more you can do, the more you can help. The more you can help, the more you can impact. Less isn't more here! More is more and money in your hands is far better than money in anyone else's hands because you have a God Money Mindset and a willingness to be used by God to build His kingdom however He may call you to.

This book is designed to give you all the frameworks I know to be true and be a turn-key blueprint of how Christian entrepreneurs can build wealth while still keeping their heart in check. This is a guide to help you navigate through your journey of building your God Money Empire to glorify God. I wanted to be able to package helpful and practical strategies that we had to learn and figure out the hard way so you could be put on the fast track to hitting your God-given potential.

I love Luke 16:10. It truly is a steward's promise. If we are trustworthy with little, we will be trusted with much. God loves us so much that He gave us free will. We can choose to do whatever we want with what we have. We can either settle and squander it or we can step out in faith and help build God's kingdom. The way I best know how to do this is by becoming who God intended you to be. Part of this is continuing to find ways to increase your income. When you have more income it frees up mental space so you can focus more on purpose. If all you have is just enough, then you can't possibly become who God created you to be because your money struggles choke out room for abundant thinking and creativity. You are unique, a true one of one. No one can do you the way you can. So let's apply these practical money making principles so you can do the work you were created for and not just the work you signed up for.

Here are seven practical strategies you can use to increase your income.

1. **Increase Your Price:**

One of the simplest ways to increase your income is to raise your prices. So for whatever service or product you are providing, see how you can make sense of increasing your price. How much more value can you add that doesn't necessarily cost you any more money— but it does need to be more valuable.

Here's an example of this: Let's say you're a freelance graphics designer who charges $50 per hour for your services. To increase your income, you could bump up your hourly rate to $75 per hour. To build value for the extra $25 charge you could create some type of guarantee for your work. Or let's say you're selling medical back braces and you normally charge $100 for the back brace. You could increase your price to $150 and create a lifetime guarantee on that product. You need to be able to add value without breaking your own bank. Get creative and see what you can come up with.

2. **Expand Your Product and Services:**

You can consider offering additional products or services that would pair well with your current offering.

Suppose you're a fitness coach who specializes in weight loss.

You could add a nutrition coaching service to go along with your workout program. Bundling products is a great way to maximize your efforts and become more of a one-stop shop for your clients so they can hit their goals and change their lives. Or let's say you are selling RVs. If your dealership had the room, you could offer two years of free storage when they purchase an RV from your team. This would remove the stress and financial burden of finding and paying for RV storage. At the RV dealership I worked for, Bretz RV, this is exactly what they offered and I know it helped close the deal more times than not and allowed for a better buying experience for the customer.

3. <u>Create A Referral Program:</u>

Encourage your current clients to refer new customers to your business by offering incentives, such as discounts or free products and services. This is something that is normally called a finder's fee or a bird dog fee. Auto and RV dealerships often have this– if you refer someone to their dealership and they purchase a vehicle or RV then you would get a $100 to $400 check for that referral. Or imagine you run a boutique shop. To encourage your current customer base to refer new customers, you could offer a discount code for both old and new customers. This would be a great way to utilize word-of-mouth advertising.

4. Offer Upsells and Cross Sells:

When customers are in the process of purchasing your product or service, you can offer an additional product or service that complements their original purchase.

For example, let's say you own a bakery and a customer orders a birthday cake. You could offer to include cupcakes and balloons as part of the "party package" for an additional markup. Or let's say you sell furniture and for an additional charge you could deliver and set it up for the customer, making it even easier for them to enjoy their new furniture set.

5. Increase Your Marketing Efforts:

Invest in marketing strategies that will help you reach a wider audience and attract new customers. This could include social media advertising, email marketing and better SEO (search engine optimization).

Say you run a small landscaping business. To increase your visibility and attract new customers, you could run Facebook ads that target homeowners in your local area. You could also offer free landscaping to a local celebrity that would be willing to create and post content on their social platforms.

6. <u>Streamline Your Operations:</u>

This is one of the most cost effective ways to increase your income. Take a look at how your business is operating; decide what can be automated or find where you can use a better process for a certain task. Making efficient changes to operations will free up time and cash flow so you can reinvest those into other areas of your business.

Imagine you run an online Etsy jewelry store. To streamline your operations and reduce time spent on administrative tasks, you could invest in a tool that automates your order fulfillment process. This would in turn allow you to spend more time creating and selling your beautiful hand-crafted pieces.

7. <u>Explore New Markets:</u>

Consider expanding your business to new markets or geographies. This could involve targeting a different demographic, offering your products and services in a new region, or expanding internationally.

For example, you run a language school that teaches English to foreign students. To increase your income you could expand your business by offering other languages like

Spanish or French. This would expand your reach and draw new clientele to your business.

Your God-given talents and abilities have gotten you this far. Now you must lean into those and become a student of who you were created to be. My whole life I've loved people. I know I'm a "people person." I love being around lots of different people. It's easy to be compassionate and encouraging towards others. I know that's one of my gifts from God. However, it's up to me to be growing within that gift. I don't believe God gave us our gifts for just yesterday, but for today and tomorrow! What are some of your gifts? What are personality traits you have that come second nature to you and you know you were born to share with others?

It's very important to be self aware and constantly take inventory of your life. I am a proud member of C12 which is a once-monthly Christian-led forum that advocates "Great Businesses for a Greater Purpose."

We start our day with fellowship, prayer, and then dive into our Balance wheels.

This is a compartmentalized wheel that includes the following:

Ranking 1-10 in each area of your life with 1 being the lowest and 10 the highest, how are you doing in the following:

Marriage/Family
-Is your marriage God centered? Are you loving your spouse unconditionally? Are you remembering to "Date" each other? How well are you communicating? How is your relationship with your kids? Are you spending quality time with them?

Personal Finances
-What are your financial goals and are you on target? How well are you stewarding what you've been blessed with?

Biblical Community

-Are you part of a small group? Are you attending church? Are you doing life together with your brothers and sisters in Christ?

Fun & Recreation

-Are you remembering to enjoy the process? Are you learning any new hobbies or are you passionate about some? Are you reconnecting with all of God's creation?

Fitness & Nutrition

-Are you taking care of yourself? How's your eating going? How active are you? Are you giving your body the proper fuel it needs to perform at the highest level?

Rest & Retreat

-Are you practicing sabbath? Are you truly resting? Are you leaning more on God than yourself?

Walk with God

-Are you reading your Bible? Are you doing life with God? How is your prayer time? Are you focused on God's purpose for your life? Are you actively pursuing God?

Discipling Others

-Are you being a beacon of light to those around you? Do people see Jesus through you? Are you pouring into others? What kind of influence are you being?

We rate ourselves on how we are doing in all these different areas of life. It's a great reminder to make sure your priorities are in the right place. It's to help promote balance so you can readjust if you get out of balance. The goal is to just continue to improve and to live out a godly life. Then there's a section that allows you to assess how you are tracking, business-wise and finance-wise.

I have a hunch most people do not do this. So before you even know you're out of alignment with your goals and your purpose, it can feel too late. You weren't able to notice any of the red flags or warning signs so now you're in a hole so deep it looks like you can't ever get out of it. This is one of the reasons I'm writing this book– to help you bring awareness to your finances and your heart's position towards money so you can avoid the entrapment of bad debt, zero financial hope, and a bitter heart towards money and business.

Purposefully assessing where you are financially allows you to develop great stewardship so you can get more and have more, while at the same time not having it affect your heart or who you are. We should try to improve daily–not only our character or our faith but also in our abilities to earn more money. Again, what is money? It's a tool that is meant to be used. By having a deeper understanding of what the Bible says about money, it will release you from the confusion that has been created in our churches and in our culture. Don't make money any tougher than it needs to be. By keeping emotion out of it, you are able to focus on God's purpose for you and your life and make a ton of money in the process.

I don't believe God wants less for you. Why would He? He's God! The reason I'm so blessed is that I know I don't deserve anything I have, and yet I still ask God for it. I understand that the things I want and ask for can only happen if God opens those doors. The things and ideas I have will only happen if God wants them to. I can work as hard as I want but if I'm not aligned with God's Word and His will, then the grind is for nothing. God wants to bless you and it's okay to ask Him for anything you want. God knows what's best for us, and will give us opportunities to become more like Him. He will always do His part, so just remember to do yours. By taking the gifts you have and continuing to develop them to glorify God, God will bless you and keep your path straight. He already gave us the ultimate gift….Jesus! So anything else He wants to bless us with is just a bonus. "Ask and you shall receive. Seek and you will find."

9 THE GOD MONEY 10% 40% 50% FRAMEWORK

2 Corinthians 9:6 ESV

The point is this: whoever sows sparingly will also reap sparingly, and whoever sows bountifully will also reap bountifully.

This next God Money Framework is how you collapse time! Time is one thing we don't have total control over. However, there are strategies and frameworks such as this that can allow you to "buy" your future time. This has been an accelerator and a secret weapon when it comes to wealth creation and the time it takes to build.

Now that you have already learned and mastered the God Money 10%20%70% Framework, it's time to take full advantage of the present and explode your ability to create wealth by leveling up to the God Money 10%40%50% Framework.

You'll notice there hasn't been a chapter called "Upgrade Your Lifestyle" yet. That's for another book.

That's because that is not important right now. This book is to help you hit Christian Millionaire Status and build your God Money Empire. I was a multimillionaire before I ever bought a brand new car. I always bought and still do buy clothes that are on sale. Building wealth takes discipline and consistency. You have to understand this sacrifice is temporary. Pay the price today so you can pay any price tomorrow.

It's amazing what God can do with your obedience and your faithfulness in just a few years. Yes, you should celebrate wins like hitting your targets and goals, but also figure out ways to do so without accumulating bad debt. Right now you should be focused on making as much money as you can and accumulating as many cash flowing assets as possible. Use your assets to pay for your luxuries later.

GOD MONEY 10%40%50% Framework:

You are still going to be tithing 10%, but instead of only 20% going into your STI account, you are now going to be dumping 40% of your earned income into that account! Yup, that's what I said, 40%. I know it might be hard to even begin to see how that could be possible. That's what I thought, too, until we were able to one day do it.

You need to trust the process and keep your faith that God will open doors for you to make this happen. This is two parts faith and one part strategy and process. You've now read two chapters hitting hard on the topic of increasing your income. Nowhere did it say "Increase your income so you can increase your standard of living." You've been sold the lie that as you make more, you should consume more. This is a worldly view on money, not a biblical one. We are to be good stewards of what we've been blessed with, so postpone leisure and luxury just a little longer so that you can set yourself and your family up for true financial freedom. You are going to live off of the remaining 50% of your earned income. The more you make, the easier this will be. The toughest part about this framework is making $250,000 a year and not being tempted to live off of the whole $250,000.

Here is an example of how this can play out. Side note, *when* you decide to implement this God Money 10%40%50% Framework is going to be heavily dependent on your living expenses and what you are willing to tolerate for X amount of time. Having clear goals and money targets will allow you to track your progress and give you a realistic picture for when you might want to splurge on something... a sports car, vacation, watch, etc.

Kelsie and I were totally on board with this when we were making around $150k. Our budget looked like this:

$150,000 Income

10% $15,000 Tithe

40% $60,000 STI ACCOUNT

50% $75,000 Live Off

We kept our living expenses at around $40,000 to $50,000 a year and still found opportunities to give more than our tithes and live a joy-filled life. Just because you are exercising these frameworks doesn't mean you are always strapped for cash and unhappy. We never felt lack because our focus was on our bigger kingdom goals rather than buying the next shiny thing. Be grateful for the discipline and be listening to God's voice when He asks you to bless others.

With the $75,000 STI account, we were able to purchase more real estate. We bought another duplex for $315,000. The rents were super low, around $700 each side, and it needed a lot of work. We were able to put in sweat equity and about $15,000 worth of upgrades.

These upgrades included the following:
-New Carpets in bedrooms
-New luxury sheet vinyl in the bathrooms
-New flooring throughout the main walkways
-New light fixtures
-New countertops
-New sinks
-New faucets
-Painted cabinets
-New baseboards
-New outlet covers
-New cedar fence in backyard
-Fresh coat of paint throughout
-Refinished bathtub

All of this we were able to get done for about $15,000. Yes, we did most of the work ourselves but we were still able to shop around and get great contractors to help. When you are starting out, it is okay to do most of the work yourself to maximize profits. YouTube is a great source for education and is how I learned almost everything I know about doing rehab.

Here are the numbers on that deal.
Duplex Sale Price= $315,000
25% Down Payment= $78,750
Monthly Payment= $1,300 (principal and interest)
Current Rents= $700x2=$1,400 gross income

After you factor in your insurance, property management fees, and an extra monthly cash amount set aside for repairs, this duplex is costing us about $200 to $300 a month. Most people would look at that and think what a waste. That is costing you hundreds of dollars a month! But I knew this was going to be a great deal! I look at real estate every day so I know where the market is and when a good deal hits.

Whatever you're into, you need to pay attention to it daily so you can become a practitioner in that field. Speed and knowledge are HUGE advantages when it comes to building wealth, especially in real estate.

I did my due diligence and it checked off all the boxes of what I classify as a great real estate deal! You can head over to www.godmoneysecrets.com to get a copy of my God Money Real Estate Checklist. I saw the market value rents were around $1,100 to $1,400 for that area and for basic amenities. So we got to work and invested $15,000 worth of upgrades and were able to get rents up to $1,295 on each side. Now this is what the new numbers looked like on this deal:

Duplex Sale Price= $315,000

25% Down Payment= $78,750

Monthly Payment= $1,300 (principal and interest)

NEW Rents= $1,295x2=$2,590 gross income

VERY DIFFERENT than a month ago when we bought the deal. Now this was a great property that had a monthly cash flow of about $800 to $1,000 a month. So by putting in sweat equity and investing $15,000 we were able to force appreciate this $315,000 duplex to a new market value price of $450,000+. That is a 15%+ return cash on cash. Again, this is why we invest in real estate! That's a $120,000+ profit created in just a few weeks worth of work. Head over to www.godmoneysecrets.com and click on Real Estate to see exactly how we did this.

By the way, an important side note is you don't need to be 100% on these God Money Frameworks. If you need to adjust a few times a year because "life happened," that's totally fine. Just know these frameworks work if you work them. They are 100% proven and anyone can do it. It's tough at first but when you start to develop the healthy habit of executing these frameworks and start to see your God Money

Empire being created before your eyes, it will pour fuel on the fire! When you can take a guaranteed formula and see life-changing results, you will be blown away by how you will be able to see more of God's abundant plan for your life.

Getting your money right and under control has more to do with you being able to focus on your purpose than just earning more money. The head space more money will buy you is priceless. Throughout life we get so focused on just trying to get by that we miss life entirely. Money is important and should be taken seriously but so should your God-given purpose. Most people aren't able to focus on or figure out both at the same time because life doesn't stop and wait for you to figure it out. So once I discovered and understood how my God Money Frameworks could drastically help change people's lives I had to share it as quickly as possible.

10
YOU ARE A ONE OF ONE

Esther 4:14

For if you remain silent at this time, relief and deliverance for the Jews will arise from another place, but you and your father's family will perish. And who knows but that you have come to your royal position for such a time as this?

"If not you, then who? If not now, then when?" -Hillel, a first century Jewish scholar
What a powerful statement.

Congratulations! You now have the God Money Frameworks and Blueprint to create wealth using biblical principles. If you just use everything I gave you in this book, you will be able to live and create an amazing life. You will be able to tap into God's abundant plan for your life. This does take work on your part and it also takes faith–faith that God will do what He says He will do.

In an amazing sermon by Pastor Dr. Dharius Daniels of Change Church, he brilliantly described three different types of faith– sour faith, safe faith, and strange faith.

<u>Sour Faith:</u>

Sour faith is when your past experiences and your disappointment of the past sour your faith for your future. It's when you allow your experiences to have more authority than what God says, than what the Bible says. You see, some of us used to want more, we used to be able to see God's vision for our life. You used to pray for God to do big things through us; however, for whatever reason, your timing and God's timing just didn't line up or what you were hoping for wasn't what God wanted for you, so your faith soured. It's having just enough faith that God will get you to heaven but it will be miserable for you on earth until that day. Yes, you are going to heaven but you have no faith for God to do miraculous things in your life. You know Jesus is with you *through* your suffering but He won't do anything *for* your suffering.

Safe Faith:

Safe faith is a limited belief. It has more to do with your own ability to do something than God's. It's more about being pretty sure you can do something but if God would just help you out a little bit then you could do it. When you have safe faith, you only set safe goals, safe targets. You aren't really believing in what God can do and what He wants to do; you are more interested in staying in your comfort zone. Are you believing in your dreams because you think they are possible or are you believing in your dreams because you know God can do it? This type of faith is more centered on protecting your disappointment than showing God's ability and character. You don't want to look silly by setting too high of a goal because you don't want to explain to others why you didn't hit your goal or your potential, so you aim low. You settle for good instead of God's best. This faith is limiting because it's based on your abilities and not God's. It becomes your prison and you aren't even able to enjoy the accomplishments because you know deep down inside God has more for you. You're unsure so you never step out of your comfort zone. And because of this you aren't ever able to step into all of what God has for you. Your fear of being let down is greater than your belief that God will do what He says He will do.

Strange Faith:

Strange faith is uncommon. It makes no sense to unbelievers. It is based on who God says He is rather than what makes logical sense. This type of faith has more to do with God's abilities than yours. This type of faith isn't free of doubt but it's knowing and acting like God is telling the truth in spite of your doubt. Impossible is what God does. Just because we can't see how He is going to do it, doesn't mean He isn't going to do it. If God said it then it will happen.

If He gave you that dream or that vision or that goal then it will happen. You have to have more faith in His abilities than in your disabilities. There have been so many times when my confidence wasn't there but my courage was because I know Whose I am and I know God can do it even if I can't see how. God wants to partner with us. "For I know the plans I have for you, plans to prosper you and not to harm you," says the Lord. He is just looking for someone who will be available for Him to use, for Him to bless, similar to the woman with the issue of blood in the Bible. She believed that if she could just touch Jesus's clothes– not even Jesus himself– that she would be healed and blessed. And what happened? As she made her way through the crowd, she reached out and touched Jesus's clothes. Jesus said, "Who touched me?" When she came forward Jesus said, "By your faith you are healed." Isn't that amazing! Isn't that a strange faith? She believed that just touching His clothes would be enough to heal her and so Jesus did just that.

Your faith is a huge part of your wealth building journey. Going back to the God Money Mindset, you have to know what God says about you and what God is wanting to do through you and with you. Yes, He wants to bless you, but He also wants you to know that He can do anything. God wants you to have strange faith. If you do, then He is able to work in ways you never thought possible. He is able to bless you in ways you never thought possible. He is able to heal you in ways you never thought possible. He is able to give you peace in situations you never thought possible. Why? Because He is God and He loves you! Now do you want to know how to have Strange Faith? Here are three principles you need in order to have strange faith:

1. Meditation on the Word
2. Limitation of negative voices
3. Impartation of the gift

Meditate:

Joshua 1:8 Keep this Book of the Law always on your lips; meditate on it day and night, so that you may be careful to do everything written in it. Then you will be prosperous and successful.

If you are always plugged into God's Word then you will be able to see and hear what He wants to do with you, through you, and for you. How can you possibly know what God wants to do if you aren't spending time with Him? How can you possibly get more from God if you aren't stewarding what He has already given you?

Limitation:

You need to limit the negative voices in your life. Yes, this may mean even those you love dearly. Family and friends can sometimes be the worst. I don't think they do this on purpose. I think they are genuinely trying to protect you. Protect you from what? Protect you from the limitations they have themselves. So their sour and safe faith will be something that they will try to push on you without even knowing it. Some people will cause you to believe less and not more. God gave you the dreams and visions He did for a reason. That doesn't mean He also gave them to those around you. He made them special for you. That's why they're yours, not anyone else's.

Impartation:

Romans 1:11

I long to see you so that I may impart to you some spiritual gift to make you strong—

Impartation is getting spiritual gifts from the Holy Spirit. When you are walking in God's will and having strange faith you might get into an opportunity where your skills won't be able to get you to the next step. So God will impart what you need, not because you're good but because God is. When He sees you faithful and obedient there is nothing you can't do without

Him. As an entrepreneur you will go through different seasons when you will need different abilities. You can rest knowing God will only give you what you can handle; He will also partner with you in the process if you have the faith for it.

Who wants strange faith? I do!

I hope by now you can see that God loves you and He wants amazing things for you. He doesn't want you to settle but He will let you settle at whatever level you choose. Just having faith isn't enough. You need to have the faith that allows God to do what He wants to in your life. You also need to apply the practical principles in this book. Life shouldn't be something we are just trying to get through. Life can be amazing every day if you so choose. My grandpa passed away many years ago; we had a picture of him in a frame that read "Happiness is for those who choose it," and I couldn't agree more. In the same way that you can choose happiness, you can also choose to be wealthy.

Wealth is predictable. You can choose to build your own God Money Empire to help further God's kingdom and have an amazing life here on earth. A version of these God Money frameworks I've given you are what the wealthy already do. If you use the same biblical principles as other wealthy Christian entrepreneurs do then you will be wealthy. Principles work for everyone. If you work the principles they will work for you.

When you are able to build wealth you are able to spend your days meditating and focusing on your God-given purpose. You want the money thing figured out so you can get to your actual work…. But I thought I wanted to be rich so I could retire? No, you want to be rich so you only have to do your work. Not your job, but your work! You see, Jesus had a *job*; He was a carpenter. His *work* was Redeemer. You never retire from your work; however, you do get to retire from your job once your money is taken care of. By becoming wealthy you free up your time and your mental capacity to have room to discover your work, your purpose. When you are working on your purpose you are able to become truly successful and live out a purposeful life, a life that God has designed for you.

Remember these God Money principles and you will find the success you were created for:

God Money Decision:

The God Money Mindset focuses on these topics:

-Partner with God

-Steward for God

-Abundance over lack

-Create over Compete

-You vs. You & God

Money:

-Love people, not money

-Use money, not people

-It's a tool

-It's a key

-Make as much as you can

Tithe:

-Tithing is a discipline

-Three different ways to give (tithe, First fruits, and offerings)

-Tithe 10% of your income (know if you tithe on the gross or the net)

-Tithing has the power to multiply everything you want and have

Snowball Bad Debt, Credit Score, Leverage Credit:

-Get rid of all your unproductive debt

-Take your credit score seriously and use it to help

accumulate assets that pay you each month

-Use productive debt to build your wealth

The God Money 10% 20% 70% Framework:

-Success can be predictable by your plan

-Tithe 10% of your income

-Save to Invest 20% of your income

-Live off 70% of your income

Increase your income:

-Use what God has already blessed you with

-Skill Stack, always keep learning and improving

-Be, Do, Have

Asset Accumulation and House Hacking:

-Look at money in percentages instead of amounts

-Use the Stay Broke principle

-Use your STI Account to buy Assets that pay you monthly

-Know your exits on deals

Increase your income again:

-Increase your price

-Expand your products and services

-Create Referral program

-Offer upsells and cross sells

-Increase your marketing efforts

-Streamline your operations and cut the fat

-Explore new markets

The God Money 10% 40% 50% Framework:

-Accelerate your wealth creation by deploying this framework

-Tithe 10% of your income

-Save to Invest 40% of your income

-Live Off 50% of your income

-Let your assets pay for your luxuries and liabilities

You are a One of One:

-You are called for such a time as this

-There are three types of faith (Sour Faith, Safe Faith, and Strange Faith)

-Only you can do you the way you can!

God created you on purpose. He made you for a purpose, to live out your purpose. You see, out of the eight billion plus people on the planet, you are the only you! You are one of one. How crazy is that? You are the only you who can do you the way you can! Read that again! You are the only you who can do you the way you can! God gave you everything you need to take your next steps. I hope you can see how this book will help compress time in your wealth building journey.

Thank you so much again for grabbing this book. If it has helped you in any way at all please let us know at www.godmoneysecrets.com. We love hearing about our community success stories and how God is moving in your life. If you would like to collaborate with me and our team, please go to the connect page at www.godmoneysecrets.com

Have an amazing life and I hope to meet you one day soon, my friend. Remember God loves you and He has big things in store for your future.

THAT WAS AMAZING... NOW WHAT DO I DO?

If you are like me, this book blew your mind! Seeing how God wants to partner up with us to help build His kingdom is amazing in itself. If you feel like this book gave you everything you needed to go live out your purpose filled life then congratulations! We feel honored to be part of your journey and can't wait to see the difference you make in this world.

However, if you feel like you got a ton of value from this book yet still need help taking your next step in building your God Money Empire then head over to www.GODMONEYSECRETS.com and get plugged into all of our amazing products and courses. We also have a GOD MONEY MAKEOVER CHALLENGE we put on once a month that you need to be a part of. We have equipped so many people through our products in helping them become who God created them to be. The world is a better place when you KNOW your calling and God given mission. Head over to www.GODMONEYSECRETS.com to find the life changing program that will help you take your next step in building your God Money Empire! We are cheering for you and know you can do it! With God all things are possible!

THANK YOU!

I want to extend my deepest gratitude to each and every one of you. Your time, attention, and willingness to explore the relationship between faith, money, and personal growth is deeply appreciated.

Writing this book has been a labor of love, and it wouldn't have been possible without your support and engagement. I hope that the words and wisdom within these pages have been enlightening and empowering for you. It has been my sincere desire to shed light on what the Bible says about money, dispelling misconceptions, and showing that money itself is not inherently bad; rather, it's our intentions and actions that determine its impact.

But GOD MONEY is not just about money; it's also about realizing the full extent of your potential as a

Christian entrepreneur and finding true success in becoming the person God created you to be. Your journey towards financial prosperity is intertwined with your spiritual journey, and I hope this book has helped you navigate both with clarity and conviction.

Remember, success is not measured solely by wealth or possessions, but by the lives we touch, the love we share, and the purpose we fulfill. Keep the teachings of the Bible close to your heart, for it is a timeless guide to living a fulfilling and prosperous life in every sense.

I encourage you to take the lessons and insights from this book and apply them in your daily life. Continue to seek wisdom, stay faithful, and never lose sight of your true purpose. You have the potential to make a positive impact on your life and the lives of those around you.

Thank you again for joining me on this journey. I wish you boundless blessings, financial prosperity, and unwavering faith as you continue your path to becoming the person God created you to be. May your faith, your work, and your finances align harmoniously, bringing you closer to the abundant life God intends for you.

Your coach, friend, and partner,
GOOSE SUSSI

www.ingramcontent.com/pod-product-compliance
Lightning Source LLC
LaVergne TN
LVHW020927090426
835512LV00020B/3243